WAY WORSE THAN BEING A DENTIST

BEING A DENTIST

(The Lawyer's Quest for Meaning)

WAY WORSE THAN BEING A DENTIST

(The Lawyer's Quest for Meaning)

WILL MEYERHOFER, JD MSW

MILL CITY PRESS

Mill City Press, Inc.

212 3rd Avenue North, Suite 290

Minneapolis, MN 55401

612.455.2294

www.millcitypublishing.com

Images are for inspiration.

ISBN-13: 978-1-937600-22-8

LCCN: 2011939549

Typeset by Sara Pokorny

Printed in the United States of America

DEDICATION:

To the Partners of Sullivan & Cromwell LLP

For all that you do.

"You varlet! You serf! You buggering knave! Yes, I swear it! E're this night doth wane, you will drink the black sperm of my vengeance!"

- from *Beyond the Valley of the Dolls*,
by Russ Meyer and Roger Ebert

TABLE OF CONTENTS

RECITALS

WHEREAS *Even* **DENTISTS** *have it better;*
Dentists don't really have it that bad.

The myth is they couldn't hack medical school, took the easy way out, and sold their souls for a lifetime of rotting teeth, retreating gums, and the highest suicide rate of any profession.

In reality - compared to lawyers (at least in terms of career satisfaction) - dentists frolic through meadows of singing daisies. Dentists romp and gambol and cavort. They cut capers. And that's an average day at the office. For dentists, life is beautiful.

Drill, baby, drill.

Lawyers are the ones who hate their jobs, and as a result, their lives. The secret of lawyer misery just hasn't leaked out to the general public. Not yet.

That's why I wrote this book. So everyone can share the news.

WHEREAS EVERYONE *hates lawyers;*
A lawyer joke:
> *Why won't a tarantula bite a lawyer?*
> *Professional courtesy.*

The whole world hates lawyers. That hasn't changed.

The big secret is that lately, lawyers also hate themselves. They hate being lawyers.

A video circulated recently through the legal community - the 2010 commencement address at the University of Denver Sturm College of Law. It might give you an idea how bad things are.

The speech wasn't delivered by Ellen Degeneres or Alec Baldwin or even Jon Stewart or Rachel Maddow. It was delivered by a graduating student whose wife and children were killed by a drunk driver in his first semester. It might have lightened the mood a bit if they'd gone ahead and invited the grim reaper.

Here are a few snatches of the speech, to give you an idea of the frothy hilarity that ensued:

"...The road ahead will not be an easy one... We face some very challenging times...Insecurity, uncertainty and constant change define our everyday reality.... 43% of private practice law firms have had lay-offs, 33% have frozen hiring, 29% have deferred start dates for new hires and 26% have reduced salaries... Compared to other professions, lawyers have the highest rate of depression and anxiety.... And it's getting worse."

Whoo-hoo! Go class of 2010!

WHEREAS *You can't make* **THIS SHIT** *up;*

A friend of mine, who used to be a senior associate at a big-shot law firm, then a partner at a less bit-shot law firm, then a legal head-hunter, then a law school careers counselor, taught me this golden rule of the legal profession: You can't make this shit up.

He's right. You can't. Unless you're a lawyer, people think you're kidding when you talk about how bad it can get.

Here's a taste of some the websites out there for lawyers:

  LawyersWithDepression.com
  MyDebtorsPrison.com
  DepressedLawyer.com
  DaveNeeFoundation.com (named after a law student who
  committed suicide; addresses depression and suicide
  among law students)
  ListlessLawyer.com
  LaidOffLawyer.com
  BitterLawyer.com
  EscapeFromTheLaw.com

As you read this book, please consider that I am not making any of this stuff up. Either I experienced it myself, or my clients experienced it and told me about it and I wrote it down. I'm just trying to keep it real.

WHEREAS *you're reading* **THIS BOOK;**

This book is not just for lawyers – but it's mostly for lawyers. The lid is coming off on the state of crisis in the legal profession – and my columns and this book constitute a first blast of truth.

This book is also intended for the people who live with lawyers – the people to whom they kvetch. The wife. The kids. The mom. The neighbors. Anyone who knows a lawyer is probably wondering what's going on and whether he's just an overpaid pain in the ass (or why he can't seem to find a job) or if there's something to all this meshugas.

There is something to all this meshugas.

WHEREAS *Who the Hell is* **THE PEOPLE'S THERAPIST**?!?;

Like all lawyers, I didn't know what I wanted to do after college, so I went to law school to get my mother off my back.

I was good at going to school. The recipient of a fellowship to a British public school and a *magna cum laude* English degree from Harvard, I sailed into NYU Law, earned good grades, published a journal article, summered at the ACLU - and wound up at a top New York City law firm, Sullivan & Cromwell.

In going to S&C, I told myself I was selling out – and I did my best to play the part. I wore stodgy suits from Brooks Brothers and toiled day and night, doing CDO deals and M&A at places like Goldman, Sachs and AIG. I like to think I contributed, in my small way, to bringing our nation's economy to its knees.

Meanwhile, I was a basket case. Biglaw was killing me. More about that later.

I finally did the impossible and escaped law, fleeing to a sweet job as a marketing exec at a dot com. Then came 9/11, and the dot com implosion.

At that point, I gave up on the business world and followed my dream to become a psychotherapist. Initially, I worked at a hospital, then opened a private practice, treating artists and poets, Williamsburg hipsters, starving actors - and very few lawyers.

I was loving life, and wrote "Life is a Brief Opportunity for Joy," a book about the importance of psychotherapy and conscious living. My agent suggested I start a blog.

From there, things moved quickly.

In early 2010, AboveTheLaw.com interviewed me for their regular

"Alternative Careers for Lawyers" column. Emails poured in. I was deluged with appointment requests.

Eighteen months later, my posts generate thousands of weekly reads and are reprinted in Chinese by a journal in Beijing. My blog is approaching one million views. In my waiting room, hipsters are rubbing elbows with lawyers.

That's my story.

WHEREAS, LAW is FUCKED;

The problem with law is that it started out as a real profession and ended up a cynical sell-out.

Things looked pretty good, at first. Young Abraham Lincoln learned law the old-fashioned way, memorizing Blackstone's *Commentaries* by candlelight, leaning on a split-rail fence - or trailing behind a hoary curmudgeon, riding the circuit on horseback, pleading countrified cases before crotchety judges.

It was folksy. It was sincere. It was old-fashioned Americana, like a leather football helmet, or bobbing for apples, or dancing do-si-do, or sitting on a porch swing and holding hands. That kind of thing.

Even with the advent of law schools, there remained something crusty and collegial and all-Ivy about law. John Houseman would peer over his reading glasses at you, testing your mettle. You needed to have what it took – grit, pith, probity, a firm chin, bushy eyebrows - to join the ranks of Atticus Finch and Perry Mason (which is what all lawyers were like back then.)

There were oaken bookshelves and tables and lumpy leather chairs and those little brass lamps with green shades. You hunched over tomes, combing mildewy pages for the smallest detail to break a case. You worked hard. You proved yourself. You wore tweed. You intoned pithily. You saved the world. You realized it was a new moon the night of the murder. The witness couldn't have seen your client out behind the woodshed because it was a pitch black night!

You also made a fair amount of money.

It sounded good. Especially to a humanities major who wandered lonely as a cloud through college, lacked the focus or commitment for a PhD - and couldn't think of anything else to do. At some point, your parents began to look at you funny, like, "is he ever going to *do anything*?"

Law school to the rescue!

The plan was foolproof. All you needed, basically, was to go back to college for three more years. When you got out, your parents would beam with pride and you'd no longer be that loser playing Grand Theft Auto on the sofa in the rec room.

You would be an attorney. A member of the bar. An officer of the court. Earning serious bank, wearing a suit, with a secretary and the whole deal. Almost like a grown-up.

Sounds good. Sign me up.

Years pass. Calendar pages riffle.

Somehow, you're not the only one to concoct this plan.

Law school classes mushroom. Law school tuitions mushroom. Law school schools mushroom.

As the schools burgeon into factory complexes (and student debt skyrockets), the firms begin to swell in size, too - then pullulate, then swell in size again, then swell in size some more. Then they throw in the towel and start wearing sweat pants all day, spooning Nutella into their mouths straight from the jar.

No more oaken bookshelves. Welcome to the cube farm.

Suddenly, it's all about the billable hour. Firms expect sixty – preferably eighty - hour weeks. They cast you dirty looks if you're not working nights and weekends. If you take a vacation, you've betrayed their trust.

Now you are a disposable drone. There is no such thing as praise – you're lucky if they notice your existence. You've never worked so hard – but everything you do is accepted with a sour frown of reproach. You are a disappointment. You are no good at anything.

Each year a new class arrives, stampeding for their chance to experience the deadening horror that's grinding you down to pulped meat.

Most people can make it two years before burn out. But you can't leave, because you have almost two hundred thousand dollars in school debt. That's *typical.*

Oh – I forgot. That was the situation a few years ago.

The legal profession is currently experiencing the collapse of an employment bubble similar to the one that popped in the academic world back in the 1980's, when so many people had PhD's in Croatian imagist poetry, Jacques Derrida's nephew couldn't find a teaching gig.

The JD is the new PhD – they're a dime a dozen.

Now you finish law school with almost two hundred thousand in debt and can't even find a hellish job at a nightmarish firm.

Just to review: you spend more money than you may ever see in your life and work your tail off for three years at not-terribly-interesting stuff so you can either hate your life as a thrall of evil corporate tyrants or sit at home, unemployed, up to your ears in debt.

That's what the majority of my clients are facing when they walk into my office, traumatized, disillusioned, weeping, searching for a way out of this hell.

At this point, the United States and much of the world sits afloat a vast effluvium – a bloody hemorrhage of unhappy lawyers.

It's a bad scene.

THEREFORE;

This book is intended to sound an alarm about the state of law as a profession.

I've tried to keep things light, but there's a serious side, too.

Something has to be done. People are getting hurt.

PART ONE:

How Did You Get into This Mess?

Magical Thinking

So many cases like this appear at my office that I'll construct him/her as a composite. That way perhaps I can spare myself the chore of receiving those - "how dare you write about one of your clients" comments that I receive every week when I get specific in detailing my fictions and some of you decide I simply must be writing about your roommate.

So here goes.

He/she is very young – 22 or 23 or 24 or 25.

He/she moved across the country to go to a law school that I've heard of vaguely. It turns out to be number 79 or 83 or 66 out of the top 100, according to some hack newspaper that profits from disseminating this sort of nonsense.

He/she is the son/daughter of immigrants from Bangladesh, Peru, Kenya, Romania or Ireland.

His/her immigrant parents operate a doughnut bakery, dry cleaner, small hobbyist shop, motel or air-conditioner repair service.

His/her parents are adamant that he/she marry someone from Bangladesh, Peru, Kenya, Romania or Ireland in a traditional ceremony - soon – and produce male children.

Before then – quickly - he/she has to become a doctor.

He/she is no good at math or science or dating, so that's not going to happen to him/her any time soon. Being a lawyer is the official second choice - not as good as a doctor, but acceptable.

He/she has just started law school at number 79 or 83 or 66 out of 100 and is presenting with anxiety around test-taking and deep feelings of insecurity about his/her abilities compared to those of his/her classmates.

We talk about CBT – cognitive behavioral therapy – to identify the thoughts that are triggering the anxiety – fears of being unable to live up to dad/mom's demanding agenda, especially when, despite getting accepted into number 79 or 83 or 66 out of 100, he/she suspects he/she has never been all that great at school. College was a struggle, too. It is possible that he/she is simply doing his/her best, but isn't cut out for academics and would be happier doing something else, such as operating a doughnut bakery, dry cleaner, small hobbyist shop, motel or air-conditioner repair service. But he/she runs from that idea – it doesn't compute with the dreams and expectations of his/her immigrant parents from Bangladesh, Peru, Kenya, Romania or Ireland.

We learn his/her parents remind him/her that they sacrificed everything for their son/daughter, so he/she could have a future. His/her parents gave up their own happiness so he/she could succeed. This notion is recited to him/her in some form or other about five times each week, most recently in the form of phone calls from home.

We learn he/she has an older brother/sister, who is a doctor, is married to someone from Bangladesh, Peru, Kenya, Romania or Ireland, and has two male children.

We also talk about the ever-widening pharmacopeia available to him/her, should he/she decide to go that route. There are the anti-depressants, which take two weeks or so to work, and have side-effects he/she might not like. There are the anti-anxietals, the benzos, like Xanax and Klonopin, which might be habit-forming. There are the stimulants, like Adderall or Concerta or Ritalin, which will help you focus on studying, at least unless you abuse them, like many law students, and stay up night after night without sleep and start hearing voices – which happened to a client of mine (no – for you helpful litigators out there - not while under my care, and no, I'm not a medical doctor, so I didn't prescribe the stuff.)

But there is another issue that I can't help discussing with him/her:

magical thinking.

Because even as he/she talks to me about his/her anxiety around being back in school, a few more facts are glossed over.

First, he/she is in the process of borrowing $170,000 which he/she cannot discharge through bankruptcy.

He/she has never seen that much money in his/her life and has no concept of how much money it is. Remember, he/she is only 22 or 23 or 24 or 25.

He/she has never worked in law. He/she only graduated from college 1 or 2 or 3 or 4 years ago, and spent most of that time working in his/her parents' doughnut bakery, dry cleaner, small hobbyist shop, motel or air-conditioner repair service.

When I ask him/her why he/she is pursuing law, I get a canned speech of the law school essay variety.

He/she wants to become an environmental lawyer/ international human rights attorney/ entertainment lawyer/ executive director of a group to help the oppressed/ federal judge.

Pressed on the details, he/she admits that he/she might have to spend a few years at a top law firm first, earning $160,000 per year, minimum. But he/she isn't doing this for the money.

Pressed to describe what precisely an environmental lawyer/ international human rights attorney/ entertainment lawyer/ executive director of a group to help the oppressed/ federal judge actually does, or how one attains these titles, things grow vague.

Pressed as to how he/she will pay back the $170,000 in loans that he/she will have accumulated at graduation, he/she looks at me like it's obvious. If you make $160,000 per year, then you need one year to pay off $160,000 and maybe another month or two for another $10,000 and it's paid off. Duh.

Oh yeah, and maybe taxes or interest or whatever - say a year and a half.

I stare at him/her. He/she stares back at me. There is a steely determination in his/her eyes. He/she isn't going to back down. This has all been arranged. It is decided.

We are at a stand-off.

5

I nibble around the edges, mentioning that paying off $170,000 might take considerably more time than that. I also suggest that getting a job as an environmental lawyer/ international human rights attorney/ entertainment lawyer/ executive director of a group to help the oppressed/ federal judge might be tough, especially given the current economic situation, and the delicate fact that he/she will be graduating somewhere in a large class from number 79 or 83 or 66 out of 100 (not to suggest that number 79 or 83 or 66 out of 100 is not a superb, horrendously under-rated institution.)

He/she tells me her professors are terrific, and she really thinks law might be interesting, once she gets the hang of it.

In desperation, I ask if he/she has ever calculated – even a rough calculation – what it costs per hour to attend one of those lectures with one of those delightful, caring, crusty old law professors. I bet him/her it will probably crunch out to about $100 - $200 per hour. For two hours each lecture. For each of the 75 students in the lecture hall.

That seems to make an impression.

I ask him/her if he/she has talked to any of the recent graduates of number 79 or 83 or 66 out of 100. He/she says there was a guy at the orientation who talked about pro bono work. He/she met another guy who graduated, not sure when, but he runs a restaurant, so he's not even a lawyer, which was weird. Oh, and a few of his/her roommate's friends are doing "contract lawyering" but he/she's not sure what that means. In any case, he/she doesn't want to do that.

I ask him/her to do me a favor, and try to find, and talk to, a few recent grads. That's it. Just talk to them.

Then I ask him/her to consider taking a year off to paralegal. For a year. Simply to see what the actual practice of law in an actual law office might entail.

He/she says he/she will think about it.

That's enough. That's something. It might be enough to defeat a little magical thinking.

Children often distort the world around them to make it bearable. If something isn't the way it ought to be for them to feel secure, they pretend it is. That's magical thinking.

If mom and dad are away all day and you're left in the house alone, you pretend you have a big white bunny rabbit who is your friend.

If mom and dad fight all the time, you pretend you can stop their arguing by being really good.

You try not to step on the cracks on the sidewalk.

When you're only 22 or 23 or 24 or 25, you're still kind of a kid inside. You don't have much experience. It's easy, under stress, to fall back into the habit of magical thinking.

But when things don't add up – maybe they just don't add up.

Borrowing $170,000 to go to number 79 or 83 or 66 out of 100 so you can become an environmental lawyer/ international human rights attorney/ entertainment lawyer/ executive director of a group to help the oppressed/ federal judge doesn't add up.

Living your life on autopilot for the sake of some misguided plan created by your immigrant parents from Bangladesh, Peru, Kenya, Romania or Ireland doesn't make much sense either.

Please. I know you're young. I know you only want to make everyone happy. But you're going to have to stop pretending the magic is real. There's a trap being laid for you. They want your money – it's really that simple. It's a scam. Please - wake up before it's too late.

You are going to have to come up with your own dreams. And you're going to have to chase them in the real world. You can't buy them with an expensive degree.

Try it. Try living your own life, your own way, with your eyes open. You'll see. It's not that bad.

You might find it's a major improvement over magical thinking.

Originally published September 22, 2010.

The Cart and the Horse

One of my clients told me last week he went to law school because he "didn't want to do an MBA." Apparently he'd only considered those two options.

Another client told me he'd decided between a PhD in History and a JD, and went with the JD because he "didn't think there would be jobs for academics." Fair enough. Unfortunately, there weren't many jobs for lawyers, either, and at least with a PhD, as opposed to law school, he might have received some sort of "stipend" (i.e., a meagre handout), or adjunct faculty position (i.e., cafeteria work.) That way, he might not have ended up both unemployed *and* in hock up to his eyebrows.

Going to graduate school has become a popular substitute for finding a job, especially in this recession. Grad school sounds easy – essentially a few extra years of college – but it only puts off a lot of tough decisions that have to be made sooner or later.

The problem here is proverbial and involves carts and horses. In a perfect world, you would explore a career and make sure it is right for you first, *then* head off to get a degree.

Instead, we have the situation I see every day in my office: young people in their mid-twenties, who grind through law school, then face not only a moribund job market, but the deeper horror of realizing they don't enjoy the work. They end up fighting to find a job in a profession they don't like simply because they have to pay off debts.

It would be great if the law schools seemed to care – if they insisted that prospective students work as paralegals for a while and make sure they know what they're getting into. But law schools are money-making concerns and they're raking in cash the way things are. They're not about to start telling the truth about their massive profits on law student tuition or the feeble job market. As they see it, that's not their problem.

What sent you off to law school, more than any other factor? Probably fear – specifically fear of being a disappointment to mom and dad. When you decided to go to law school, you saw only two options – graduate school or loser-dom. In law school, you would be doing what you'd done your entire life – going to school, which always kept your parents happy in the past. It seemed like a no-brainer. And in your early 20's, things that happen a few years from now (like paying off student loans) seem far away - they take place in another universe with another person cleaning up. Hey, plenty of people go to law school and they do whatever, and it works out, right?

Now, in many senses of the word, your loans are being called in.

One of my clients says he wishes he'd gone the burn-out route, stayed home and smoked weed. He has buddies from college who drifted after graduation. Some are working retail jobs, or in restaurants. Some have office or sales jobs. Mostly, they're blowing off work and playing in bands and part-timing as ski instructors during the winter or hanging out and talking about that back-packing trip to Bhutan they really want to do some day.

From where he's at - an unemployed quasi-lawyer waiting to hear whether he passed the bar exam while he processes the reality that he doesn't like law - being a burn-out sounds pretty good. As a burn-out, he wouldn't have loans, so he could *afford* to spend the whole day dissecting the lyrics to "Paranoid Android."

I'd like to suggest a "third path" - an alternative both to the mindless lemming-march towards graduate school and complete burn-out. It's called "finding your way on your own" and it's how people (back in some mythical, golden, halcyon olden days) used to figure out what they wanted to be when they grew up.

First, relax and don't worry if you're not making a lot of money. You're young – there's time for that.

Second, don't rush into grad school. If there's something you're dying to be when you grow up, and you absolutely have to go to grad school to get

10

some letters after your name in order to do it – then fine, go. But wait until you know where you're going before you board the train.

Third, take a look at the world around you, and get some real-life experience. Instead of borrowing money to go to grad school, you might try living cheaply at a low-paid starting position in some industry that catches your eye.

Low-paid starting positions – or internships – aren't much different from grad school. You get exploited financially, in hopes that further down the line it will help you win a job. With a starting position, instead of some useless degree, you get practical experience and a line on your resume.

While I was in law school, feeling superior, two of my friends from college struggled through lowly internships.

One was a temp, answering the phone for a clothing company. She now runs the place, reporting to the owner. Last year, when I ran into her at a party, she was heading off to Milan and Paris to hit the fashion shows.

The other friend took one of those humiliating barely-paid starting positions at a publishing house. She's now a senior editor, hobnobbing with famous authors.

Those two put the horse before the cart, and got somewhere.

Meanwhile, I put the cart before the horse, and I'm not even a lawyer anymore.

If you just graduated from law school and are sitting in a law firm right now struggling to pay off debt - or unemployed and wondering what you're going to do – this advice might be coming a little late.

But it might also explain how you ended up in this pickle – and give you some ideas for how to get out of it.

I know plenty of lawyers who realized law school was a mistake, managed eventually to pay down debts, then brushed themselves off and headed in a new direction – and found happiness and success, too.

There's always a Plan B - a way to have fun and get yourself someplace you actually want to be - if you calm down, stop worrying about what other people think, and remember that enjoying your life is a primary goal, not just an option.

Originally published September 8, 2010.

Extremely Versatile Crockery

For the record, a law degree is not "versatile." Being a lawyer amounts to a strike against you if you ever decide to pursue another career.

So why do people keep insisting it's an "extremely versatile degree"?

A bunch of reasons.

Law schools are in it for the money. Teaching law doesn't cost much, but they charge a fortune – made possible by not-dischargeable-in-bankruptcy loans. That makes each law school a massive cash cow for the rest of the university. Money flowing into the law school pays the heating bill for the not-so-profitable Department of Neo-Structuralist Linguistics.

Law students play along with the "extremely versatile degree" farce to justify the three years of their life and the ungodly pile of cash they're blowing on a degree they're not interested in and know nothing about. This myth is also intended to calm down parents. You need a story to explain why you don't have a job, but that it's somehow okay.

No one else cares. And that's chiefly why this old canard still has some life left in it.

Time to put it out of its misery.

Why is a law degree not versatile?

Let me count the ways.

For one thing, it costs about $170k. Anything that leaves you nearly two hundred grand in a hole is not increasing your "versatility" - it's trapping you in hell.

For another thing, studying arcane legal doctrine for three years (a purely arbitrary number) leaves you with no translatable skills. The arcane legal doctrine you learn in law school isn't even useful at a law firm, let alone anywhere else.

And let's talk about the "skills" a lawyer "hones" in his "profession."

A litigator is about the worst thing you can be if you want to do anything else. Why? Let's examine the skills you "master" as a litigator.

Pumping up billables. Dragging out discovery. Dreaming up and laboriously penning pointless motions to create delay. Behaving in an oddly aggressive and hostile manner at meetings that end in a standstill. Organizing complicated information into folders, and folders of folders and labeling everything and organizing that into lists, and lists of lists, then billing for it by the hour. Researching recondite issues and writing memos you're not even sure you understand. Wrapping your head around Byzantine procedural rules and forum and jurisdictional niceties and arbitrary court filing deadlines, all so you can trip up the other side with needless delay and expense.

Okay. Now translate those skills into the real world, where people make products and sell useful services.

See my point?

If you're on the corporate side, at least you get to watch business people do their thing before you spend the night typing it up. That's why corporate partners are considered more valuable at firms when it comes time to recruit. Corporate guys hang out with business people, so they bring a "book of business" (i.e., customers) with them. A litigator doesn't even have clients, just cases, which might (God forbid) end some day. A litigation partner without a live case is dead wood awaiting pruning.

Sorry.

Of course, the actual "stuff" of corporate law could drive you mad. Studying securities law is like learning the rules to the most boring, complicated board game ever invented. All you want to do is quit playing and go home.

But there's a bigger, broader problem with switching careers when you

14

have the letters JD after your name: people hate lawyers.

Why do they hate lawyers? A bunch of reasons.

If you are a real person in the outside world, the word "lawyer" means obstruction. The phrase "run it past Legal" means you might as well give up, 'cause it's never gonna happen. Exciting business ventures ooze to a standstill like a sabre-toothed tiger in the La Brea Tar Pits. Some risk-averse dweeb in a suit will spout dire warnings to you about unlikely contingencies until nothing seems like it's any fun anymore.

Lawyer means pretentious – socially awkward losers with fancy degrees telling you what to do when they've never run a business in their lives.

Lawyer means threats. "You'll hear from my lawyer" is the worst thing you can say to another person. And lawyers love to write threatening letters – it's what they do best. That's why lawyer is synonymous with wasted time and wasted money.

Lawyer means annoyance. Lawyer means hassles. Lawyer means a total void of common sense. Lawyer means expensive, with little to show for it.

Now mail someone in the real world a resume that says "lawyer" all over it and ask yourself why you never got called in for an interview.

When I was trying to escape from law I hid my law degree at the bottom of my resume, in small print. At the top, I made the most I could of a year spent managing a small, independent bookstore.

I was trying to get a job in the marketing department of a major online bookseller.

I got lucky. The guy who hired me was a former banker, who talked his way into his job by stressing experience in the credit card business. Ultimately, the two of us created the co-branded Barnes & Noble.com MasterCard.

He was willing, as an ex-banker, to understand how badly I wanted to be an ex-lawyer, and I sweetened the pot by taking a 45% pay cut and doing my own legal work (which saved him about half his departmental budget.)

I also begged, and came very close to breaking down in tears. It isn't easy convincing someone in the real world to hire a lawyer.

A year later I tried to get a friend - another burnt-out lawyer – into a job in my department. I took his resume to the head of HR.

She looked at me, uncomprehending.

WAY WORSE THAN BEING A DENTIST

"This guy's a lawyer," she said, like it tasted bad.

I flashed a winning grin. "C'mon Brenda," (HR people are always named Brenda and always have big hair.) "A year ago I showed up here with the same exact resume and I got hired."

She didn't smile.

"I wouldn't have hired you with this resume."

Then I realized why it took my boss so long to finalize my hire. He fought for me, and ended up pulling rank to get past HR.

Versatile my ass.

Look - I'm not telling you anything you don't already know.

Psychotherapy is about owning your thoughts and feelings.

Own this: A J.D. is not a versatile degree. Law is a specialized field which carries a heavy stigma beyond its own hermetic confines.

An "extremely versatile degree"?

That's simply a crock. A versatile crock. But still a crock.

Originally published November 3, 2010.

Stay Away from the Pet Cemetery

There's a terrific opening scene in Stephen King's novel, "Pet Sematary."

I don't read a lot of Stephen King novels - not because I dismiss his skill as a writer, but because they scare the hell out of me.

In this one, the main character is a young doctor. He's on his first day at a hospital when a college kid is rushed into the ER. The kid was hit by a car, so he's all smashed up, his neck broken, blood all over the place, one eyeball hanging out – whatever. Just as the doctor is concluding he's dead, an arm shoots out, grabs the doctor by the collar and the dead kid stares at him (with his working eyeball.)

"Stay away from the Pet Cemetery!" he intones.

In a flash, it's over. The kid is stone cold, and the doctor wonders if he was hallucinating.

The suggestion to stay away from the pet cemetery, however, is a sensible one. Like most sensible suggestions, it goes entirely unheeded.

I don't want to give away the ending (and I only read the first 20 pages because I got scared) but I suspect, if he stays away from the pet cemetery, flesh-eating zombies won't become an issue.

But he doesn't listen!

Lawyers are the same way. They just don't listen!

Here's another scary story. My client was in law school. With a big smile, she announced to her journalist boyfriend she was accepting a job at the big, prestigious law firm where she'd summered the year before.

He grabbed her by the collar, his face etched with horror, and intoned: "But you hated that place. It totally weirded you out. You said you were pursuing public interest. Why would you go back there?"

She didn't listen. Now their relationship is over, and she's hating her job and her life and weeping in my office.

"Why didn't I listen?"

But she's not the only one. You had moments like that, too – didn't you? When someone tried to warn you?

My Pet Sematary moment came the summer before I started law school.

I was visiting home, went to a party and ran into an old friend – a guy I'd known since I was about twelve years old. I casually related the big news - I was going to law school! I expected one of several possible reactions:

1. an expression, feigned or otherwise, of happiness that I was finding my way forward in the world;
2. a tinge of jealousy that he was still a burn-out art student while I was on my way to wielding staggering corporate power; or
3. curiosity about law school and how he might follow in my tracks.

I didn't get any of those reactions. I got disappointment and concern.

"It doesn't feel right. Please - you're a good guy. Think hard before you do this."

I didn't listen. I knew "selling out" was part of "growing up." I was acting like an adult, getting serious for a change. This guy – a computer geek interested in being an *artist* – knew nothing about my future as a high-powered corporate lawyer. He was probably jealous.

In reality, he knew a lot. He was a few years older and had friends who did the Biglaw thing. He knew the scoop, and spotted me as a train wreck waiting to happen. He also knew it was pointless to try to stop someone firmly committed to self-destruction.

Stay away from the pet cemetery!

Why is it so hard to listen, respectfully, when someone who knows you well, and knows what he's talking about, tries to warn you law might not be right?

Part of the answer is that lawyers tend to be loners. You're smart and competitive and you do it yourself. You're probably young, too, when you make the decision to pursue Biglaw. Young lawyers are eager to please, to find success and gain attention. They're not known for an eagerness to listen to others and take advice.

People resist psychotherapy for the same reason. There's the thought - "what's this guy going to understand about me or my situation I don't already know?" That's the first barrier to overcome - accepting you might need another person's feedback to discover something useful about yourself. It's not only about trusting a therapist, either. In group psychotherapy you learn that a collection of strangers might have a lot to tell you. They can spot things you miss in your own world.

A basic tenet of psychotherapy is that we need one another to heal. Opening up and listening to other people, tolerating their feelings and taking in their feedback, is a step towards maturity.

Nowadays, when someone tells me to stay away from the pet cemetery, I sit up and hear him out. I wish I'd learned that lesson sooner - it might have saved me a whole lot of trouble and wasted time.

Stay away from the pet cemetery!

Don't turn up your nose at good advice. It wouldn't kill you to give it a listen.

Originally published on March 2, 2011.

Someone Likes a Quitter

I spent the second year of my social work internship working at a community center, which offered one of the top smoking cessation programs in the country.

One fine spring day I was sprawled, sunning myself, on a bench in the courtyard of the center. A fellow intern, sitting nearby, lit up a cigarette. I proposed she give the cessation program a try.

"No one likes a quitter," she quipped, exhaling a cloud of toxins.

Uh...huh. Except there's a proviso in that statement – a "carve-out" in the contract language - covering the quitting of something self-destructive. Like smoking.

Or a pointless march through law school.

I'd like to speak in defense of quitting, and quitters.

Quitting can be about more than stopping whatever you're doing. It can be about waking up and asking yourself if what you're doing makes sense and is worth continuing.

If you're plugging away dutifully through the legal education process with no real idea why - it might be time to quit.

Does this mean I'm seriously advising young law students all over the country to give up and drop out - simply abandon their legal education mid-way through?

Yes.

I am prescribing a mass exodus from law schools. A semi-mass exodus might do the trick.

Tune in. Turn on. Drop out.

If you don't know why you're there – and you're not sure what you're getting yourself into – if you're not at a top school, or even if you are, and your grades are a little iffy, and likely to stay that way - then please, get out. Today. Before you spend another cent.

The legal education scam works because it follows two key rules of all successful Ponzi schemes:

First, it plays to your greed. You dig your own hole because you're in it for the money.

Second, it keeps you distracted. You never realize you're getting fleeced.

The process is like a cattle chute. From the LSAT to the bar exam, you never look up because you're moving too fast, racing to compete against the others...right up to the bolt gun in the forehead. Even if you awakened midway and realized you weren't having fun and wanted to flee, there's no obvious route of escape. That's how it's designed.

Along the way, you sign documents to borrow the purchase price of a Rolls Royce Corniche, with nothing to show for it but a piece of paper saying you're theoretically prepared for a job you know nothing about.

You end up almost $200k in debt and either stuck in a field you never understood and don't like - or unemployed (the unemployed part isn't the problem since it turns out you really want to be a jazz drummer anyway, not a lawyer.)

But that almost $200k in debt is there to say – sorry, you work for us now. In fact, we own you – own your future. Just like that cow on the feedlot.

You don't have to go out like that.

Last year a sweet little 24-year-old Jewish 2L from one of the dozen or so legal factories of learning in the New York metropolitan area arrived at my office with the news she was quitting school. She wanted to talk to me first. She said she felt guilty.

I'm Jewish too. I know from guilt. It's a sacred gift of our cultural heritage – but it's no reason not to quit law school.

She told me she didn't see the point of sticking around. She didn't enjoy law, her grades were so-so, and her friends who recently graduated were dealing with terrible workplace conditions and/or unemployment. She's already $50k in debt – and to her credit, at the age of 24, she seems to have an inkling of the years it will take to pay back that relatively minor insult to her finances.

Her parents support her decision. Her mother is an accountant, so she sees the importance of avoiding debt. She also seems to realize there are plenty of other, better choices for a bright, eager 24-year-old.

When I asked the 2L what she actually wanted to do when she grew up, she told me she loved clothes, and dreamed of working at her favorite chain, where she could happily wear almost anything, right off the rack. She'd have to start at the bottom, at a store, and work her way up, but she had some fight in her, and a little imagination. She was ready.

Her mother liked the idea. Lo and behold: a cool mom.

The 2L's plan was to quit school right away, but she wanted to see me first, and make sure she wasn't missing something.

She wasn't. There was no point in waiting until the end of the semester. A month in law school costs something like three or four thousand dollars. That's a lot of new clothes.

She quit last week. With my blessing.

Madness? Think again.

This 2L is cutting her losses – saving the next $150k in loans, not to mention another two years of her life that could be spent acquiring priceless real world experience in fashion retail.

She's no longer living a fantasy of graduating, jumping into a big law firm and making $160k per year. She's abandoned that pipe dream.

The new plan is to start at the bottom (where, with all due respect, 24-year-olds belong), and earn an honest wage in a business she enjoys. If she's as good as she thinks, she could work her way up to management in a few years' time. Eventually, the money she saves on legal tuition could come in handy if she decides to go back to school for an MBA or a fashion merchandising degree - but that's a ways down the road. She's smart enough to know you don't pick up the important stuff in a classroom. In the meantime, she's looking forward to the challenge of proving herself.

This 2L was different. She got it. I don't know why, but she did. Maybe she's a harbinger of good things to come. I hope so.

If reading this column makes you stop and think about staying in law school, I've done my job.

If it triggers a mass exodus of 2L's waking up and realizing they're losing that hankering for the bolt gun in the forehead, it might be the start of a movement.

No one likes a quitter?

This isn't about quitting anything – at least anything that matters.

It's about getting started leading your own life.

Originally published May 4, 2011.

Bizarro World

I summered at Shearman & Sterling way back in 1996. To judge from my clients' feedback, the summer associate "experience" at big law firms hasn't changed much over the years. With the recession, it's harder to get a summer associate position, but once you're in, it's pretty much the same old thing – or maybe the same old thing on lysergic acid diethylamide. It was a pretty weird experience to begin with.

As a summer associate, you're entering Bizarro World, and nothing makes sense in Bizarro World. Nothing ever has, and nothing ever will.

Here's how it works:

You show up, dressed in the new suit you probably bought with your mom. You're a little nervous and eager to impress. The first day starts out pretty much as you'd expect, with human resources spiels – "trainings" - on stuff like how to use the library, how to turn on your computer, how to find the word-processing department, whatever.

You are presented with your desk – your own desk in a law firm! You chat excitedly with the other summers, sizing one another up, seeking allies – someone you can trust, who seems to be thinking the same things you are. There are no obvious candidates.

Eventually you are introduced to a senior associate and given your first assignment. You rush off to finish it and promise yourself it will be the best summer associate assignment in the history of the firm. As you get down to work, it turns out to be some confusing research question that either has an obvious answer that you find in about twenty minutes, or it's not really a question at all, it's just a broad open-ended request to poke around for cases, so you're not sure what they want. Or it's an inquiry regarding the income taxation of irrevocable charitable annuity trust stand-by provisions on preferred equity warrants in the State of Florida under provision b(7) (iii), and you're feeling a little out of your depth.

Either:
You finish it in twenty minutes, with a sinking feeling in the pit of your stomach that maybe you did something wrong. So you wait an hour or two, re-checking everything, then poke around the library trying to look serious and busy before you hand it in.

Or you struggle through dozens of cases, trying to find something relevant, with a sinking feeling in the pit of your stomach that maybe you're doing something wrong, but determined to produce a good heap of print-outs and some sort of summary even if you suspect you might be totally off-point.

Or you try to figure out what a charitable annuity trust is and stand gaping like an idiot while the punctilious and efficient law librarian produces state law documents that appear to be written in Klingon. A cold wave of panic rolls up your spine. You wonder if it's worth the risk to ask the senior associate for more guidance.

Let's say you actually go back to the senior associate. You brace yourself to look like an idiot. You knock on his office door, and he's surprisingly friendly,

"Ummmm...I'm not sure I understood the parameters of the question. Do you think I could walk through it with you for a minute?"

He smiles, and too-quickly agrees that the question was a little unclear, but says it looks like you did a great job of "taking a stab at it." He admits he's busy at the moment, and suggests you put it down for now, but adds that you've "done a great job" and he'll have another assignment for you soon.

That was your first assignment and you're sure all you've accomplished is to make the one guy you needed to impress think you're an idiot.

You wait at your desk. You try not to look like you're surfing the internet, and settle for reading the New York Times online, which seems an improvement over Facebook. If you hear anyone out in the hallway, you pretend to read a memo about the "events" that have been planned for you during the summer.

Okay, if it's sometime during the past few years, there are a couple of other things. There are fewer "events" planned for you, and fewer of them involve visits to country clubs.

You also poke around the office and realize that half of the floor you're on is empty. Just empty offices. That's especially weird since there are two of you summers stuffed into a tiny office on the other side of the floor. This situation will never, ever, ever be discussed by anyone under any circumstances.

Your officemate appears. She turns bright and perky when she sees you, which is scary, since that's not how you're feeling, but you brighten up and turn perky yourself since she is.

You want to ask how her assignment went, but she's already rearranging pencils on her desk and looking intent on something, and you just know she handed it in, flawlessly executed, probably to the managing partner. He accepted it with smiles and a congratulatory handshake.

It gets to be five o'clock and you're trying to look busy and not like you're glancing at the clock every ten minutes. You wonder if you're supposed to go home now. It's kind of boring sitting here and you're hot in your suit. You imagine changing into a t-shirt and having a beer and watching tv. It seems preferable to sitting in Bizarro World wondering if you're already in trouble on your first day.

You hope your officemate will take off first. In desperation, you make for the bathroom, thinking that might give her an opening and then you can leave and no one will have to feel awkward.

The next day you get in at nine and realize no one else makes it in that early except the secretaries. You sit at your desk. Finally, you walk past the senior associate's office and sort of wave at him and let him know you exist. He waves back, but doesn't invite you in.

Your boredom is relieved by a "summer associate training breakfast." The bubbly summers are greeted by a kindly-looking older partner, who then quickly disappears. A bright, perky consultant from WestLaw or someplace like that takes over, and shows slides about legal research or insider trading or diversity sensitivity or ethics. It is boring, but there are bagels and muffins laid out on a table in the back and at this point you're happy that time is being killed.

Eventually you go back to your desk and rearrange your highlighters and post-it flags for twenty minutes. You're wondering if you should go bug the senior associate again when, to your amazement, the bright, perky young blond woman in the suit with the pearl necklace who works for human resources – or "associate development" - or whatever they call it – comes by your office asking if you want to go out for lunch.

She might not actually be blond or wear pearls. She might be African-American or older or a guy. But whoever she is, she will radiate an aura of blondness, suit-ness and pearl necklace-ness. You can't quite put your finger on it. But she is very very nice and always remembers your name, and there is nothing she wants more than to take you and a bunch of your summer associate buddies out for lunch. The best description you can think of for her job is "cruise director" and you half expect her to herd everyone onto a boat and sail you all to Martha's Vineyard, which is probably where she was born and raised.

After a few weeks, you realize this "let's all go out for lunch" thing happens a lot. Like every week. You are constantly pigging out at Italian restaurants with the other summers, who talk about NCAA basketball – not your thing – or chat mindlessly about how nice this partner is or how wacky and fun that associate is. These partners and associates are people you've barely met, so you can safely assume the other summer associates, whom you barely know, have barely met them either.

Every two weeks, you receive a paycheck for more money than you've ever been paid in your life. You notice you're getting fat from all those lunches.

The entire experience culminates in a dinner at a country club in Westchester. You've never been to a country club and aren't sure what to make of all the wealthy, skinny young second wives and blond mop-top second batch kids eyeing you by the pool. You drink too much at dinner and fall asleep in the van coming back to NYC. You say goodbye to the blond lady in the suit with the pearl necklace. You visit your family, and dodge questions about the job - and then you're back in school again, wondering what that surreal experience was all about and trying to process the notion that you might actually *work* at that place next year.

You're back from Bizarro World, but it's only a respite. Because Bizarro World is where you're headed back to soon, if you're lucky. It could become *your life*.

How you like them apples?

Years later, when it does become your life, you realize:

- Those senior associates were "assigned" you against their wills, and dreaded concocting assignments for a useless summer when they were having mindless work dumped on them and hating their own lives.
- The firm had just laid off half of its real estate department and the entire structured finance group and partners were screaming at one another at partner meetings and threatening to de-equitize under-producers, including the kindly-looking older partner, who hasn't brought in a client in twenty years, which is why they stick him with the summers.
- They were trying to lease out the extra floor to save money, but the downtown commercial real estate market is in collapse so it's sitting empty, while the partners argue.
- The senior associate you reported to was sleeping with the blond lady with the pearl necklace, although they're both married.
- No one there (except the blond lady with the pearl necklace) even remembered your name, and they will decide whether to hire you based entirely on whether there is enough business for them to bill you out for sixty hours per week at five times what they're paying you.
- Half the partners in the firm are secretly planning to jump ship to another place where the money is better and leave the other half – who aren't pulling in the billables – up a creek.

You receive a letter informing you that your hiring date has been postponed to December, earliest.

Welcome to BigLaw. It only gets more Bizarro from here.

* * *

The original publication date for this piece was June 8, 2010. I was surprised, afterward, to receive so many comments testifying to how the summer associate experience hasn't changed an iota since my time. I got the usual nostalgic stuff from older lawyers sharing a laugh at the old days – but plenty of young lawyers wrote in as well, saying I'd nailed the bizarre mood that surrounds summer associates at a big firm. I suppose some things never change. On the other hand, I got a bunch of comments from younger lawyers complaining that they never got offers to summer at firms. In a down economy, such luxuries are becoming scarce.

Not a Knuckle-dragger

I received this timely and topical letter a few weeks ago:

Hello,
Now is the time of year when all the 3L's at every law school are enjoying
the time between graduation and starting their bar review (at least for me).
Do you have any advice for us on how to keep our sanity during this 10 week
adventure and not go crazy or over-stress when the big day finally comes?
Thanks,
NewJD

It got me thinking about my own bar exam experience – and brought
back a memory from my law school days.

Close to graduation time, I was having a final meeting with a professor with
whom I'd written a journal article. It was a pleasant meeting – the article was
in print and he was pleased with it. He even said he was going to use it as part
of his syllabus for a seminar. I was feeling as close to a super-star as I ever got
in law school.

At some point I confided my concerns about the approaching bar exam.
I told him it gave me butterflies in my stomach.

"Oh, don't worry about that," he assured me. "Only the real knuckle-
draggers fail the bar."

We shared a laugh, I shook his hand and left his office, but I knew - more
than anything in the world – I needed to pass that exam. I didn't want to

be a "knuckle-dragger." I'm guessing you don't want to be one, either.

The bar is a weird exam. It goes on forever, deals mostly with trivia, and no one cares how you do on it – you only have to pass.

In real world terms, the bar exam is entirely useless. At best, it gives you a smattering of details from state law. At worst, it's downright bizarre. I remember blowing a practice question because, it turns out, "smoke-damaged," but not "charred" wood didn't count as evidence of arson in NY State. The wood had to be burned by a flame - or something like that. I stared at the answer, wondering how anything so impossibly obscure could make it onto a statewide, standardized exam. But there were plenty of questions like that.

Anyway – first, here's my exam-taking advice, handed down from my old roommate at Harvard, who went to Columbia Law School and got his JD a couple years before me. My psychotherapist advice will follow.

The trick to studying for the bar is not to bother with bar review lectures – they are a waste of time. Just take all the study materials and give yourself four hours to study them every weekday morning, from 9 am – 1 pm, for about three or four weeks.

Read the outlines front to back, slowly and carefully, then do all the practice tests, and outline each and every one of the practice essay questions. Check everything, make sure you understand anything you got wrong on the practice tests and - voila! You'll do fine. In fact, you'll be over-prepared, which is the idea.

At some point you'll realize you know everything – even the bar exam only covers a discrete universe of information. I was so over-prepared that I spent the last few days before the exam hanging out at my cousin's beach house, relaxing. By that time, I knew what I needed to know and it was getting repetitious.

If you employ this method, you will most likely follow in our paths and do extremely well on the bar exam – better than you have to do.

For years now, I've shared this advice with friends and clients. To a man, they have rejected it.

One client, last week, said "that's not going to happen."

I asked why, and she said "because I could never do that."

Now I'll put my psychotherapist hat back on, and talk about the infantilizing effects of legal education.

The entire law school process, and the profession itself, is extremely competitive. Everyone is competing with everyone else to do basically the same thing.

No one wants to be a "knuckle-dragger," so you play it safe, and do what everyone else is doing.

Your fear of being singled out as a failure, especially on the last big event, the bar exam, is so terrifying it regresses you into a child, who collapses into helplessness. So you sign up for bar review and vow to do whatever they tell you.

I'm scared. Hold my hand. Walk me to lecture, spoon-feed me the material. I'll be good. Promise me, if I do everything you say, I'll pass.

Bar review isn't that different from law school itself. Going to lectures in school is a waste of time, too. It would be more efficient to teach yourself the same material.

I knew a guy first year at NYU who skipped lectures. Instead, he bought commercial outlines, did the reading, and outlined old exam questions. It took a lot of nerve to break the rules like that and follow his own instinct, but it paid off. He got straight A's and transferred to Yale. If I had law school to do again, that's how I'd do it – like a grown-up.

The problem was that I was too scared back then. I wanted reassurance that if I did exactly what I was told I would be okay – I wouldn't be a knuckle-dragger.

Sure – we all learn differently. If you like watching a long, drawn out lecture instead of reading the same material out of a book, be my guest.

On the other hand, if you have trouble staring at something complicated in a book, figuring it out on your own and writing about it – well, I'm sorry, but that's what lawyers do for a living. They don't sit in lectures being spoon fed material by kindly professors charging two hundred dollars per hour.

Most of the people who fail the bar exam aren't really knuckle-draggers. They're students who take the regression to child-like helplessness to the extreme. They employ wishful thinking, pretending that if they go through the motions of child-like obedience – show up at each and every bar review lecture and sit quietly doing what they're told – they will automatically pass.

That's not going to happen.

You have to actually address this material as an adult, on your own terms, and learn it.

Another major reason why people fail the bar is that they create an unconscious distraction. Suddenly, just as you're preparing for this exam, you have the big breakup with your girlfriend and have to stumble around staring into the middle distance muttering fragments of French poetry. That sort of thing.

If you don't want to take the bar, don't take it. But make that decision consciously – don't design an unconscious distraction to hide that you're terrified to face this very adult challenge. People break up, or sustain whatever personal life upset comes their way, and they still pass the bar exam. You just contain your feelings and focus on the matter at hand.

Why would you regress into helplessness or create a distraction to avoid studying for the bar?

Probably because you're afraid, deep down, that you're not very good at this stuff.

It's worth at least posing the question: if you're terrible at this sort of thing – memorizing masses of dull material and spitting it back out in a lightly re-processed form - why are you pursuing law? You're only going to get out there and find yourself reading reams of not-always-scintillating material, then turning it into memos, briefs, contracts and the like.

The all-too-common answer is "because I have loans to pay off." That answer reduces you to a helpless indentured servant, working off your debts to purchase freedom.

If that's why you're taking the bar, it's no wonder you're not really into it. But you might as well own your feelings, so you can try to contain them, and get on with the task at hand, which is a lot of dull memorization and the endless grind of practice tests.

Don't worry - if you fail the bar, it doesn't mean you're a knuckle-dragger. But it might suggest you're not acting like a fully aware, autonomous adult.

Originally published May 26, 2010.

Mental Health and the Bar

I received an interesting and important letter a few weeks ago from a 3L (I've redacted it to preserve anonymity):

Mr. Meyerhofer,

I have a question (or perhaps a topic suggestion for a post, as I'm sure many students are wondering about this) about the character and fitness part of the NY bar application.

I have seen a therapist several times over the years for issues relating to depression, eating disorders, and self-injury. On the NY bar application it asks whether you have any psychological issues that might affect your ability to perform as a lawyer. I have absolutely no idea whether I'm required to disclose my psychological treatment history, or if I do, how much of it. Is the determination based on what I personally think, or is it a reasonable person standard?

As I've had to go to the ER several times over the years, objectively I could see how someone could interpret that as something that could affect my performance. However, I personally don't think that it does.

I don't really know who I could ask about this, as I don't really want my school administrators to know about my issues. Any information you might have would be much appreciated. Thank you so much for your help!

Sincerely,

"Stumped in Syracuse"

To begin with, here is a passage from a pamphlet, entitled "Are you fit to be a Lawyer," published by the New York State Lawyer Assistance Trust (www.nylat.org):

Neither receiving treatment for alcoholism, drug addiction or mental health concerns, nor the status of being a recovering alcoholic or recovering addict are grounds for denial of admission to the bar. In New York, the focus of the inquiry is on whether chemical abuse or addiction or a mental health condition impairs the applicant's current ability to practice law.

The bar application asks whether the applicant has "any mental or emotional condition or substance abuse problem that could adversely affect" the "capability to practice law", and whether the applicant is "currently using any illegal drugs."

While honesty in disclosing past conduct (for example, arrests and convictions) is essential, disclosure of past treatment is not required. No questions are asked about past treatment. The Committees encourage law students who are experiencing drug, alcohol or other addiction or mental health issues to address those issues as soon as possible, regardless of when the student plans to seek admission to the bar.

The bottom line seems clear – there's no legal duty for Stumped in Syracuse to disclose his past history of treatment on his bar application unless his mental illness currently impairs his ability to practice law. Under this standard, it would require a severe mental health condition to trigger this duty, and the majority of situations involving mental illness – certainly the ones described in Stumped in Syracuse's letter - would not require disclosure.

The real issue here – as Stumped suggests - is stigma. Stumped, like any rational person, is afraid someone will find out about his condition and jump to the unfair assumption that he is unfit for his job. That would be a disaster for anyone interested in preserving his professional reputation. For Stumped, the ignorance surrounding mental illness may pose a greater threat than the illness itself.

For whatever reason, physical disabilities don't attract the same stigma as mental illness. There are plenty of lawyers who use wheelchairs, live with seizure conditions, are deaf or, like the former Governor of New York State, David Paterson, legally blind. These attorneys require special assistance to overcome their disabilities, but they are universally accepted as competent professionals.

Lawyers battling issues of mental health deserve the same treatment. If you can overcome mental health and addiction issues to pursue a successful career, you are every bit as worthy of our respect as someone arriving in court in a wheelchair or using a Braille device.

There are thousands of practicing lawyers living with mental health and addiction issues. I know, because as I therapist I've worked personally with dozens of them. I can tell you they have enough to deal with already – they don't need the further pressure of an unfair stigma, and the constant fear of being exposed and ostracized for their condition.

If you are a lawyer dealing with an issue of mental illness, you are probably doing what anyone else in your situation would do. You preserve your confidentiality by trusting the knowledge of your condition only to trusted friends, you seek professional help - and then you take it day by day, show up at your job, and do your best.

Maybe you are working with a therapist to overcome the crippling pain of depression.

Maybe you are battling an eating disorder, like bulimia or anorexia.

Maybe you are in recovery from alcohol or drug abuse, and drop by an Alcoholic's Anonymous meeting each night, to count another day and recommit yourself to sobriety.

Maybe you are dealing with mood fluctuations resulting from a bipolar condition, and have to check in with a psychiatrist each month to adjust your medication.

Maybe you have a suicide attempt in your past, and work hard each day to overcome the impulse towards self-harm and to remind yourself of everything you have to live for.

Maybe you battle anxiety, and struggle with panic attacks or phobias that can take you by surprise and leave you shaken.

Despite these disabilities, like every other practicing lawyer – you wake up every morning, put on your suit, and do your job.

37

For that, you deserve respect.

If mental illness can't stop you from pursuing your profession, there's no reason to let ignorance stand in your way.

Originally published March 31, 2010.

Get a Job

I've written a fair amount about lawyers at the office in this column.

Right now a lot of lawyers - including some right out of law school - aren't at the office. They're at home, out of work.

Unemployment is tough on lawyers because they tend to be pleasers – they have to be, to earn the grades to make it into law school. It's all about pleasing others at a firm, too. You submit to the whims of a partner and work around the clock. Like all pleasers, lawyers get used to looking outside themselves for affirmation of their worth.

When you're unemployed, there's no one to please but yourself. You're alone with you – and for a pleaser, that can lead to a plunge in self-esteem. That's why, during unemployment, you have to be especially good to yourself. You can't afford to fall into a hole right now - you need to stay strong. That means reminding yourself of your achievements – your grades, your degree, your accomplishments at a firm.

If things get truly dire, remember the bottom line: You're doing your best. That's all anyone can ask.

This is no time to beat yourself up. Remember to be *you* – your best self - the person you really are. That's more than just a lawyer – that's a person. Spend time with friends, and people who like you. You're worth something and you know it – and you need all the support you can get.

You also need some time off. The worst thing about being unemployed, as one of my unemployed lawyer clients put it, is that "when you're unemployed, you're always working." Unemployment can turn into a 24 hour a day grind. Give yourself permission to relax sometimes. Activity is important – but so is taking time off to get your head together.

Job interviews, in my experience, can be particularly difficult for lawyers. Pleasers never learn to sell themselves – you just do what you're told and hope good things happen. That doesn't work in a job interview.

Law school offices of career services arrange mass interviews with law firms – or they used to, back in the boom years. These typically consist of a handshake, a dutiful glance at a resume, and a pointless chat about nothing. Those aren't real job interviews, or they didn't used to be. The firms were hiring resumes - they just wanted to make sure you could dress yourself. The interviewers often seemed as clueless as the candidates.

It's different now, during a recession. You have to sell yourself actively. That can be tough for a lawyer.

Here are a few basic rules:

First, a job interview is a sales presentation. You are not relating to a friend, or a mentor or a parent or teacher – or even someone who particularly cares about you. You are selling to a customer. There's a tendency for interviewees to regress under stress, and fall into unconscious patterns of behavior, like relating to a parent-figure. But that's not what a job interview is about.

An interview is not a confessional. This is not where you open up and share your truth.

If you are asked about your previous job, and you hated it, don't say so. Never lie at an interview – but don't spill your guts, either. No one wants to hire a complainer – even if your complaint is legitimate.

Stay upbeat. You have two simple messages to communicate:

(1) You can do this job; and
(2) You want this job.

That's it. Never stray from the outline.

First message: You can do this job.

An employer narrows the field to the most competent applicants. He is hiring you to do something he doesn't want to do himself. He doesn't want to teach you, or mentor you, or be bothered with you. He doesn't particularly care about your career – that's your business. He cares about his career. His worst fear is that you will screw something up and make him look bad.

You must assure him you can do this job – and won't create hassles.

Second message: You want this job.

Of the pool of competent applicants, an employer will choose the one who wants it the most. That's more than just the human instinct to give someone what he wants; he also knows you'll work harder if you appreciate having the job. He doesn't need attitude. If you can look an interviewer in the eye and say it would be a privilege to work at his firm – do so.

That's it. Communicate your two messages and get out of there.

Unemployment isn't fun, but it might make you stronger. People grow under adverse conditions – it draws out your strengths. Affirm your belief in yourself and get down to business, and you can nail that interview and get the job you want.

Confidence comes from within. It's there, if you look for it.

Originally published April 20, 2010.

Hipster. And Lawyer

Two guys from my high school. One year apart.

Hipster...and Lawyer.

Hipster plays in jazz band with Lawyer. They have the same academic advisor, and fall into a casual friendship.

Hipster has trouble in school. He plays drums and guitar, but struggles to maintain grades. It's nothing to do with behavior – everyone likes him. The academic advisor does his best, but after failing a few courses, Hipster's expelled. He ends up bouncing from school to school, and manages to graduate, then heads to a halfway-decent state university known for partying. He spends most of his year there jamming with his buddies and soon drops out. They start a rock band, smoke dope, wear tie-dye, collect Grateful Dead tapes and call each other "dude."

Lawyer thinks it's a shame Hipster got kicked out of school. His own grades are A's. He wins academic prizes, a scholarship to study in England, and advanced placement at Harvard, where he graduates magna cum laude. He heads to a first-tier law school, and places near the top of his class. An offer arrives from a white shoe firm.

Stop the tape.

We know what happens next:

Hipster acquires a beer belly, loses the tie-dye and winds up working in a call center. He moves into his old bedroom at home and turns morose. His parents mumble excuses about dyslexia.

43

Lawyer makes partner and earns a million six. He purchases a loft in SoHo, a little country place upstate and a vintage Porsche. His parents seek opportunities to smugly mention his doings to their friends, who hate them for it.

Here's what actually happens:

Trey Anastasio's jam-band, Phish, becomes an international success. He plays sports stadiums and records with Herbie Hancock. He's worth millions. His parents are pleased.

Lawyer – *that's me!* - sinks into abject misery at Sullivan & Cromwell, and gets the shove after his second year. I do a lot of psychotherapy, change careers a couple times, and become The People's Therapist. I don't make much money. My parents are relieved I'm not a depressed lawyer anymore.

My point: Being a pothead jam-band guitarist might be a better way to get rich than becoming a lawyer. Especially if that's who you really are, and being a lawyer isn't.

It's a rare thing to get rich. It has to be - rich means you have more money than everyone else.

If you want to get rich, you have a choice. You can do what you love and hope lightning strikes. That worked for Trey. Or you can sell out and go where the money is.

If you're banking on the second option, know this: Being a lawyer is a lousy way to get rich. Law puts you in massive debt, and lawyers are poorly-paid compared to finance types and sometimes even accountants. Also, thanks to the almighty billable hour, you end up working around the clock.

Many lawyers wind up gazing across the divide from lawyer to hipster with a twinge of regret. Their "burn-out" friends might flounder and muddle along from job to job, but eventually, as a hipster, you'll probably find yourself, get your act together and emerge from the experience without debt. You also get to wear tie-dye, sleep late, smoke awesome weed, and call people "dude." You might even find your soul.

Lawyers burn out a lot. That's when you realize you need some time to flounder and muddle too – but by then you owe almost $200k to a bank, so even if you hate law, you have to stick around to pay off your ransom. That kills more years, in addition to the three already consumed by law school.

You lose the critical years Hipster spent finding his groove. Essentially, you sacrifice your twenties – an essential decade for floundering and self-discovery.

Everything isn't rosy for Hipster - all that floundering and muddling can take its toll and it doesn't always wind up like a fairy tale. But Hipster accomplishes necessary work towards personal growth. He's allowing the play side of his life to express itself in his choice of work - and every once in a while, Hipsters turn into rock stars. That's because, when you do something you love, which speaks to who you are and expresses your passions, you tend to get good at it.

As a therapist, it isn't my job to change anyone – or to tell you what to do. My job is to create awareness of your own your thoughts and feelings, so you can get yourself where you want to be.

But consider becoming a hipster.

* * *

Originally published April 6, 2011. No, I'm not close friends with Trey Anastasio, although I'm sure he'd recognize me if we ran into one another at a reunion. We liked each other well enough in high school, but didn't spend much time together. I was moderately obsessed with Jerry Garcia and the Grateful Dead, but by the time Phish was getting big I'd fallen into a jazz addiction and wasn't catching a lot of rock shows. Also - yes, I know, if Trey fits any category, it's probably "hippie," not "hipster." But hippie sounds dated and Trey's too cool to be labelled a hippie. I wasn't sure what else to call him. "Phish leader" would have spoiled the reveal.

PART TWO:

The Hell that is Big Firm Life

No Longer in Kansas

There's one thing every lawyer, no matter how miserable, seems to agree on: law school wasn't that bad. In fact, it was kinda fun. Things take a nosedive when you get to a firm - that's when you start hating life.

Let's take a look at this phenomenon, and ask ourselves why that's the case.

There are a few prominent disparities between the experience of law school and that at a big law firm. Right off the bat, in law school when you work hard, you get a reward. There is an "incentive" for "doing your best." I remember a guy in my class at NYU who used to grow an exam beard every semester. He'd stop shaving a couple of weeks before exams. The beard would start to get scraggly – then, after the last bluebook was filled with scribble, he'd shave it off and everyone would hit a bar to celebrate. It was silly, light-hearted fun, designed to focus attention on completing a goal.

Contrast that to a law firm, where nothing is silly, light-hearted or fun - and there is no such thing as completing a goal. At a firm, you don't "complete goals." Thanks to your massive student loans, you are now someone's property, and you work to avoid punishment. That means you work until midnight, then go in on the weekend. Rinse. Repeat. There is no end of semester. There is no end of the week. There is no end of anything. There is no vacation. There is no end. Your reward for working harder than you've ever worked in your life? If you do a good job, no one complains – and you get more work.

That is, unless there isn't any work, in which case you're in trouble, because that means you're not going to make your billables, which means you're a parasite and a useless drain on the firm and you should feel terrible about yourself and fear for your job.

It's also possible that you didn't do a very good job on whatever it was you were working on harder than you've worked on anything in your entire life. That might be because you've been working eighty hour weeks with no vacation and receiving a steady stream of criticism, all the while fearing for your job, which is a problem because you have a wife who wants to have a kid and you're $180,000 in debt. The Zoloft and Klonopin your shrink prescribed don't seem to be doing the trick. Nor does the Adderall you're popping with alarming frequency – the left-over Adderall from the first shrink, who diagnosed you with ADHD before the second one decided it was actually depression and anxiety.

It might be that all the other work you did for the past six months at the firm was good, or even very good - until you handed in this latest assignment, which wasn't good. However, at a law firm, if you do something that isn't good, it doesn't matter if you did one hundred other things that were good. You did something that wasn't good, which means you are bad.

The reason this thing wasn't good might be that you had no idea what you were doing because they gave you something unbelievably, insanely, laughably complicated to do over the weekend with a totally inadequate explanation.

That brings me to a second way in which law firms are not like law school.

In law school when something's complicated, you study it slowly until you understand it. The professor will point out that the Erie Rules, for example, are tricky, and note that it may take a few weeks – or most of a semester – to navigate these treacherous waters of legal doctrine.

That doesn't happen at a law firm. The only time anyone takes a good long time to explain something to you at a law firm is during one of those CLE classes, where they kill half a day on the same "legal ethics" material you learned back in law school, when it was painfully obvious and boring the first time around. That, they spend hours on.

Then you return to your desk, where there's a voice message from a partner, who wants a lengthy research memo done over the weekend on the tax consequences of the securitization of synthetic reverse-flip butterfly debenture-backed double interest-rate insurance SWAP options denominated in Swiss Francs, if held, pre-fiscal 2007, under a dual-indemnified Barbados limited partnership irrevocable trust.

Actually, he'd like something emailed to him by Sunday, so he'll have time to look at it before he meets with the client on Monday morning. This is a client you've never met and never will meet. In fact, you're not sure who the client is, since you don't usually work for this partner. You're not even sure what this deal is about. You're not even sure if you remember exactly what a "derivative" is, especially since it's Friday at 6 pm, and you are officially supposed to be a first-year real estate associate except that, due to the financial collapse, there no longer is a real estate department. Before you do anything you have to cancel your trip home this weekend for your little sister's bat-mitzvah and listen to your mother deliver a guilt trip. Then you have to stay up all night in the library, sorting through financial arcana about a deal you don't understand. Then, relying heavily upon the miracle of Adderall, you have to apply recondite legal principles to a hazy fact pattern while trying not to fall asleep or burst into tears.

In law school, answering this research question would constitute a semester's work in an advanced seminar and probably result in a journal article. You would be a super-stud if you got a B in the course.

At the firm, pretty much whatever you hand in – even if written in your own blood – will be received with disdain as "not up to snuff" and "poor work product" and you will be asked if this is really the best you can do and it will be hinted that "maybe you aren't cut out for this place." If you are fired, you will never be quite certain if it is because of this assignment or simply because the firm is imploding and you're being cut along with half the other associates and three partners, who were originally supposed to work in the now non-existent real estate department.

In short, if law school is a pleaser's vision of heaven – then law firms are the pleaser version of Hades. Instead of kindly law professors handing out A's at the end of the semester, there's a partner who considers you a chattel. He's not handing out anything, unless you screw up, in which case you will get your ass handed to you.

The "semester" ends when you're laid off, fired or suffer a mental and/or physical breakdown.

You've seen the look on the first years' faces when a month or two goes by, it's no longer the summer program, and they start to realize they're in it for real.

They're not in Kansas anymore.

* * *

I was surprised by the reaction from readers to this piece, which was originally published October 20, 2010. Instead of objecting to my hellish depiction of law firm life, I mostly got letters from people saying they hated law school, too! Everyone else wrote in to say, yep, that's how it is at a law firm...proving once again I don't make this stuff up.

Fighting Back from a Bad Review

My client, a senior associate doing IP litigation at a downtown firm, brought me the bad news.

"I got a terrible review last week."

She seemed calm about it, considering. That's because she knows how law firms work.

"I'm expensive, and they're preparing for lay-offs. So they told me I'm terrible. It was ridiculous. They made stuff up off the top of their heads."

I had to hand it to her. I wish I could have been so cool when the same thing happened to me.

My first year review at Sullivan & Cromwell went fine. Mostly, they didn't seem to notice I existed - I wasn't important enough to review. Then, in the second year, it was suddenly a horror show. Nothing I did was right. The partners don't fool around at S&C – they give it to you with a sledgehammer. Even at the time, I remember wondering about that one partner who seemed to like me. Of course, he wasn't mentioned at the review.

Years later, after I'd given up on a legal career, I realized the truth. They probably gave identical reviews to ten or fifteen percent of my class that year. It was a lay-off, and we were the ones who got cut. Those terrible reviews were the partners' way of creating a paper trail in preparation for letting us go – covering their tracks in case we sued.

My client, an experienced senior associate at her second law firm job, knew how to handle this sort of thing. You don't let them throw you.

She admitted to feeling shaken when she walked out of that office, and for a few days she didn't tell anyone about it – just kept the feelings inside. It was painful, after all the late nights and hard work, to hear them say terrible things about her, and initially it triggered feelings of shame. But she caught herself, and managed to snap out of it. She called me for an appointment, opened up about the ordeal, and decided then and there she would call a headhunter and start setting up interviews. She was resolved to get out of that place ASAP and go someplace else, where she would be appreciated for the work she did.

Unfortunately, for every cool customer like that client, there are about a dozen weeping young over-achievers who show up at my office utterly devastated by this sort of review. They've spent their entire lives at the top of their classes in school, bringing apples to delighted teachers – and suddenly they fail to please.

A few months ago I listened sympathetically to a fourth-year associate who'd received the review from hell. He was bemoaning his inadequacy as a human being, when I decided I'd heard enough and spoke up:

"You went to Yale. You were in the top fifth of your class. You did litigation at Cravath before you even showed up at this firm. You're a brilliant classical pianist and a smart, interesting, terrific guy. When did you suddenly become incapable?"

Something began to creep back into his face. It looked like self-respect. All I'd done was remind him who he was.

Don't fall for the bad review routine. It's a crock. And it can hurt you. When you are beaten up like that, but don't feel you can fight back, the anger can turn inward and devastate your self-esteem, creating depression. That pattern can lead to self-punitive behavior and even suicidal thoughts.

Stop that process before it begins. Enforce a self-barrier, a piece of emotional insulation between you and those evil partners. You might not always be right – but you aren't always wrong, either.

A balanced review is just that – balanced. It is the job of managers to motivate you by pointing out your positives as well as your areas of weakness. If they don't, you have to fall back on your own self-knowledge,

and belief in who you are. Never lose hold of that.
You know who you are. You know what you can do.

Originally published February 24, 2010.

A Sick and Boring Life

There's a scene in John Waters' classic film, "Female Trouble," in which Edith Massey, playing Aunt Ida, begs her nephew, Gator, to give the gay lifestyle a chance.

Gator, poor thing, refuses, which sends Ida into pleading desperation. Here's the dialog -

Gator: Ain't no way; I'm straight. I like a lot of queers, but I don't dig their equipment, you know? I like *women*!

Ida: But you could change! Queers are just better. I'd be so proud if you was a fag, and had a nice beautician boyfriend... I'd never have to worry.

Gator: There ain't nothing to worry about.

Ida: I worry that you'll work in an office! Have children! Celebrate wedding anniversaries! The world of the heterosexual is a sick and boring life!

Sometimes I feel that way about the world of law.

For the record, I'm not trying to change anyone's sexual orientation here, or even suggest that it could be changed – that's not what this scene is about. The absurd humor in Gator and Ida's exchange derives from Waters' inversion of the normal situation: parents are supposed to nag you to be straight, not to be gay. Just like they're supposed to nag you to get a job and work hard and act like an adult and get serious about your life and go to law school.

But a lot of the time I feel like Aunt Ida - pleading with lawyers not to get

57

serious and buckle down, but precisely the opposite - to give something –
anything - wacky and fun and subversive – or merely indecorous - a chance.
That's because, if you're not careful, slaving away at a big law firm can drain
all the spark out of life, leaving things looking...well...sick and boring.

Now and then, after I receive a new referral, I succumb to the temptation
to Google that person's name. The first few times I did this, it was to find out
whether he or she was male or female. That happens sometimes – you get an
email from "Pat" or "Jamie" or "Oyedele," and set up an appointment, then
aren't sure what to expect.

The inevitable result of an online search, in the case of a lawyer, is a
page from a law firm directory. You get a passport-size photo capturing
the flannel-suited subject with a slightly shocked deer-in-the-headlight
expression, then the inevitable list of schools attended, bar admissions and
a capsule summary of obscure "practice areas," all rendered in lawfirm-ese:
"General Practice Group," "Corporate Capital Markets Restructuring,"
"Derivatives Litigation and Regulation." There's no sense of an actual
person in those pages - only a scary apparition from the world of the serious
and very grown-up. I still recoil, looking at those bland, comically formal
law firm directory pages – just as I wince looking at my old photo in the
Sullivan & Cromwell facebook.

In the case of a new client referral, that passport photo comes to life a
few days later in my office, in the form of an unhappy person confessing
his loathing for his firm, bemoaning the steady stream of abuse, the sterile,
alienating culture, crippling hours – the usual lawyer misery.

I wonder how ordinary people can be split in two like that, transformed
simultaneously into the miserable, suffering human being sitting in my
office, while the outward appearance is meticulously maintained – that
official law firm image of a ring wraith from the world of the humorless.

Then I remember how S&C worked its magic on me, embalming me in
its parallel dimension of un-fun.

It begins with the physical plant. Like so many big law firms, you enter S&C
through an ugly Mies-ian knock-off modernist skyscraper, only to emerge
from the elevator in an Ethan Allen showroom. The removal of all color
from your world can have a subtle, but powerful effect – and S&C fetishized
colorlessness. Beige wall-to-wall carpet drowned all sound. The walls were

lined with a featureless beige muslin that further muffled vital signs. And then there were the ubiquitous hunting prints – someone must have raided every antique shop in Connecticut, acquiring en masse a thousand dull watercolors of someone or other "running the hounds."

The lunchroom conversation was stunningly narcotic, too. If you sat with partners, you had a choice of topics. There were the relative merits of leasing or renting your Jaguar/Land Rover/BMW. There was the eternal furor over Scarsdale property taxes. If you got lucky, you might be privileged with cryptic references to sports events, interspersed with mumbled shop talk.

Seated with the associates, if you were unlucky, you could get trapped in one of those conversations about hours. I spectated at a few of these pissing contests, in which so-and-so bravely admitted he'd billed 30,000 hours that month alone, and such-and-such countered with how that was nothing, he'd billed 50,000 hours that very week, habitually sleeping in his office, eating each and every meal at his desk.

To this day, I have refused to bother calculating how many hours per day a thousand or two thousand or three thousand hours per month or year or whatever it is actually works out to. My sense is that people should either work for someone else from around nine to around five – or they should work for themselves, whenever they want. Anything else is sort of nuts.

How sick and boring did things get at S&C? I remember debating with my boyfriend whether it would be too "risky" for me to wear a blue shirt to work – rather than a more conservative white one. That, of course, to accompany one of my two Brooks Brothers' suits and feeble collection of striped ties.

The first step for many of my clients is restoring their personalities from the long, deep sleep of law firm anesthesia. It's fun to watch. Suddenly, that woman in the charcoal grey suit shows up in a t-shirt and jeans - and confesses a crush on L.L. Cool J. That permanently spooked-looking guy begins to relax and rhapsodize about his early days at U. Mich, drinking chianti, talking philosophy and playing banjo. It's like the door to the crypt slides open, and out emerges...an actual living, breathing person.

If you're going to work at one of those big law firms, you can at least refuse to drink the Kool-Aid and remember who you are. It took me weeks, after realizing I would be departing S&C, for warm blood to creep back into my veins. It helped to play a cd of Bach's Well-Tempered Clavier over and over in my office for a few weeks. There was something about ethereal music that worked like a cross in one of those exorcist movies. You might have to find your own brand of garlic to hang over your office door to repel the soul-vampires. But you'll need something.

Listen to Aunt Ida. Lighten up, break some rules - have a little fun. Otherwise, you could find yourself leading a sick and boring life.

Originally published October 6, 2010.

Call of the Wild

I'll never forget a moment in a wildlife program about Antarctic penguins – I think it was a David Attenborough series.

There were two little penguin parents and a penguin chick.

Then, suddenly, there wasn't. The chick fell into a crack in the ice.

The little guy squeaked for all he was worth, the parents circled, there was frantic waving of wings - and not a damn thing anyone could do.

Five minutes later – which seemed like several lifetimes - a member of the film crew tore away a chunk of snow and released the chick.

Profound relief for all involved, penguin and human.

But there was a wrinkle. The show's non-intervention policy had been violated. A voice-over explained that an exception had been made because the film crew may have created the crack in the ice.

Uh, yeah. I doubt David Attenborough was buying that story.

The truth? You try filming a baby penguin slowly perishing in front of its parents.

One of my clients, a Biglaw senior associate, experienced something similar.

The situation: An 8th year associate – not my client - was up for partner. She worked at a branch office of a huge firm. My client was preparing a case for trial, and her team needed help. They sent word to the branch office, which sent the 8th year. She showed up bright-eyed and bushy-tailed, but the partner - an unstable sadist - decided on a whim after two weeks that this 8th year was no good. He didn't tell her to her face. Instead, he mocked her behind her back to the entire team, proclaiming her work product worse than a second year's, and bragging he'd send her packing to the branch office, where she belonged.

My client watched all this, and felt complicit. She wasn't laughing, but she wasn't saying anything either.

It was like watching the baby penguin.

This 8th year had no idea she was the object of ridicule. In fact, she was arrogant – confident she'd make partner. At the branch office she was their pride and joy, and they sent her to the big city to win support for her bid.

That bid was being derailed. One word from the partner to the branch office and Miss 8th year's aspirations were toast.

There was nothing wrong with the 8th year's abilities – she just wasn't used to the level of aggression this partner demanded in his written work. That, and the partner wanted to hurt something small and helpless.

My client's instinct was to step in and warn the 8th year.

She didn't.

Maybe the penguin analogy isn't quite right. This 8th year was hardly a helpless baby penguin - she was a cold-blooded litigator. If she were watching this happen to someone else, she wouldn't intervene either.

A better analogy might be gazelles on the African savannah, watching as a hungry lion paces nearby. Each gazelle knows how things are going to end – one of them will be lunch. They would prefer it be someone else. They eye the others – that one's old, that one's lame, that one's still a fawn.

The lion makes the same calculation. He chooses a weak runner, and gives chase.

The other gazelles flee, knowing he'll get his meal. But this time, it's not them.

My client was afraid of this partner. If she warned the 8th year, it might get back to him – and that wasn't worth the risk. There was nothing she or any of the other gazelles could say to the lion – or to one another – that would do this 8th year any good. She was marked. The others were already stepping out of the way. Nature would take its course.

But the lion and gazelle analogy might not be apt either. Gazelles are harmless, but at a law firm anyone can turn dangerous. My client wasn't naïve. She knew, if this 8ᵗʰ year came to power, she would grow fangs and learn to kill.

A friend of mine recently returned from Australia. He was amazed to find nearly every living creature that walks, swims or crawls Down Under can turn out to be deadly poisonous. It was incredible, he said – they had venomous toads and frogs and spiders and fish and snakes and centipedes and jellyfish and even a poisonous octopus. Just about anything you met could end up killing you.

What was it about living isolated together on a desert island that turned everyone poisonous?

I was reminded of the comments section on AboveTheLaw.

Of all the websites run – or formerly run - by Breaking Media, only one regularly triggers comments that might have been penned during a break from sewing a dress made of human skin.

As a columnist for Above the Law, I have been told not only that I suck and my pieces are too long, but that I am an "anal rapist" and should "die in a fire."

That doesn't happen when you write for Fashionista, Dealbreaker, or (formerly) Going Concern – let alone Alt Transport.

Fashion people, Wall Streeters, accountants and alternative transportation wonks like their jobs. They like where they are in the world.

Lawyers turn vicious because they hate their jobs. They don't want to be there.

If you are stranded on a miserable island with the same people for a long time, eyeing one another as candidates for lunch, you begin to turn poisonous. Everything turns poisonous.

You watch the damn penguin die, and you're glad it's not you.

It starts to feel like a law firm.

Originally published January 26, 2011.

The Angel and the Devil

There comes a time as a lawyer when you split in two – an angel and a devil. The angel wants to do well - as I never tire of explaining, lawyers are pleasers. You want to make partner, earn a million bucks and be the best attorney in the world. To the angel, the firm is like your high school football team – go Skadden! Rah rah rah!!

The devil, on the other hand, would burn the place to the ground while he toasted marshmallows and sang campfire songs.

The irony is that it's the law firm itself that turns little angels into devils - just by telling you that's who you are.

A junior partner at a big firm told me how they did it to him. Two senior partners marched into his office and announced he was slacking off and taking advantage of the firm. It was a mistake, they told him, to make him partner.

In reality, this guy was a pleaser's pleaser. He worked his ass off to make partner, and talked in all sincerity about his "gratitude to the firm for that honor." He was as rah-rah as it got.

Unfortunately, none of that meant anything, because the economy sucked, and he wasn't bringing in billables. According to firm logic, that meant he wasn't trying, he didn't care – he was a bad guy. By the end of his grilling, all he wanted to do was slack off and go home. They'd done it – turned an angel into the freeloading devil they told him he was.

A few weeks later, he's still having trouble finding his groove, and feels tempted to fudge his hours, pad his expenses, and kick off early. It seems reasonable, all of a sudden, to glance at a document and hand it off to an associate to review instead of staying that extra couple hours at the office.

There are few things quite as frustrating as having someone question whether you are acting in good faith. It's like one of those Hitchcock movies where they collar the wrong guy for a crime he didn't commit and no one believes him when he insists he's innocent.

Law firms do it all the time.

At Sullivan & Cromwell, it got to feeling like a roller coaster. I arrived at the firm fresh-faced and innocent, totally committed to doing my best. I know how absurdly naïve it sounds now, but I really did think I had a chance of making partner.

You couldn't get more angel than me. I spent three years earning A's in law school, pleasing professors, drinking the Kool-Aid, writing a journal article, drinking more Kool-Aid, talking about my commitment to "the profession" - all the while whipping up flour-less Kool-Aid gateau served with mint-rosemary Kool-Aid coulis.

Come to think of it, maybe that's why I'm so bitter now – why lawyers are all bitter – because we bought in utterly at the start of things. We really were angels. It's a long, hard fall to the shadowland of Hades.

My expectations for Sullivan & Cromwell were ridiculous, in retrospect. I perceived the partners to be wise, caring mentors who would guide me to "excellence." I bragged to everyone I met about where I worked, employing words like "collegial" to describe my vision of the firm. No kidding - "collegial."

My plunge to the land of shadows only truly arrived when they ignored all that and accused me of being a slacker. It was their telling me I didn't take my work seriously that somehow made it a reality. There's something about working your ass off only to be told you're a slacker that actually turns you into a slacker. Suddenly padding your hours and avoiding work become the prime objective. Let the other little junior – Mr. Eagerness - handle things for a change.

A few days later, I'd snap out of it and remember why I was at S&C. It was the best, most prestigious law firm in the world! I wanted to make partner! I was going to make them happy, do my absolute best, and be a success!

Then I'd get stomped on by some senior associate telling me I didn't even seem to care...and the process would begin again.

At some point, you go numb. (Even lawyers have their limits.)

In the end, you stop cycling back and forth. You want out.

I worked, as a therapist, with a burned-out third year associate from a mid-sized Mid-Western firm who told me she was quitting her job. I urged her to reconsider. It looked like the firm was going to fire her anyway. The head partner kept threatening to let her go if she missed their insane billable hour requirements. She'd been denied vacation for nine months and was on the verge of mental and physical collapse. They kept telling her she wasn't committed to the firm's success and was slacking off and avoiding her responsibilities.

I proposed a classic slacker strategy to milk the firm for money:

"Why don't you hang on a bit more," I implored her. "You can take all that vacation they owe you at once. If they refuse to let you have it, you can make a scene – or stop working hard. One way or the other they'll fire you. Then you can collect unemployment insurance, which would help you keep up your loan payments while you move in with your parents and look for another job."

She sighed.

"That's not how I want to go out."

She explained that she'd never - not once – tried to take advantage of that place. She operated in good faith from day one, and did her very best. She'd done well in law school and never worked so hard in her life once she arrived at the firm. She always played by the rules, and wanted to leave still playing by the rules. She doubted they'd fire her – they'd probably just dump work on her, then criticize her for it ("your work-product is not up to our expectations...") announce she hadn't made her hours, then dump more work on her, and use her poor reviews as an excuse to once again postpone her raise. Standard procedure. No one lasted more than three years. Now she knew why.

"I can't walk back into that office. I hate it too much. I hate them too much. I'm leaving."

It was useless to argue. She'd had enough. She'd tried to be the angel. She'd battled the urge to become the devil, even when that was who they told her she was – and practically forced her to be. Now she was fed up, burned-out, numb.

She's looking into a career as a literary agent.

Enough is enough.

Originally published November 17, 2010.

Alone in a Crowd

Last week I did a first session with a typical client - a young lawyer worried about starting at a big firm.

I couldn't do real psychotherapy with this guy. Some lawyers are like that - they don't trust anyone enough to open up. It was more like an awkward coaching session. When I tried to explore his feelings, he cut me off and got down to business.

He was fine, he assured me. He'd already decided he was going to take the money. He just wanted some advice. Then he related bad experiences from the summer program, and asked for my take on big firm life.

I suggested ways to maintain emotional insulation from the worst aspects of a big firm. I also proposed that he do psychotherapy, and maybe group psychotherapy, for emotional support while he was there. This didn't make much of an impression - his mind seemed elsewhere.

He mentioned wistfully that he "wanted to be a writer, but couldn't make a decent living at it." I waited for more, but he changed the subject.

Eventually he left my office, and I thought that's that. I'd never hear from him again – another unhappy lawyer who'd contacted me in a moment of weakness, then retreated back to his cave, alone.

The next day I received an email that pretended to be a thank you, but was really a warning from this guy not to mention his story in my column. It was a curt, condescending note which ended like a law firm letter, with "best regards." Only a lawyer could write a note like that to a therapist.

I've received a few of these threatening notes over the years. I consider them a by-product of working with lawyers.

I know what you're thinking. Yes, I'm a therapist, and I charge people for my services. And of course I disguise identities in this column to preserve confidentiality. He has a right to send me any letter he wants, and to have his confidentiality preserved.

But there's a larger issue here. Trust. And sharing. And honesty.

My column, and my work as a psychotherapist, are intended to help people. I work with plenty of clients – many of them non-lawyers – who open up to me and find relief.

It's always tougher with lawyers. They hesitate to trust anyone. That makes things harder for me – but incalculably harder for them.

Big firm attorneys live in a closet. Inauthenticity is the rule at these firms – it pervades the culture. No one admits what they're feeling because no one is supposed to trust anyone else. The result is isolation, which exacerbates every other toxic element of that life.

It's a kind of macho code: Act like you're doing fine, no matter what.

One of my clients said she broke down in tears last week in the bathroom stall at her firm, after a partner tore into her for some screw-up. She chose the bathroom because of her firm's "open door policy." She wasn't allowed to close her office door for privacy.

I asked her how everyone else at her firm was holding up.

She shrugged.

"Fine, I guess."

According to her, about two-thirds of the associates were fleeing after three years. I doubt they're all doing fine.

Lawyers are good at hiding things. Especially how they feel.

Once in a while, I receive a letter or comment on my website that says: Mr. Meyerhofer, here's my story. I want to share it so others know what I've been through.

It would be nice to receive more of those notes – and fewer threats. I'll probably receive a letter this week from someone complaining I wrote a column about him.

You're so vain. You probably think this column is about you.
But this column IS about you: all of you. All of you, my fellow lawyers.

I listen to unhappy lawyers all week long. Then I receive stern messages commanding me not to tell anyone else what's going on out there. That's ridiculous.

If you're feeling the way you're feeling – someone else is too.

Don't let them isolate you. Take a risk and open up. Walk to the office next door, sit down, and talk to a colleague. Compare notes. Share your experiences.

That's what you do in therapy - take the risk of being present, and speaking your truth.

It's no great secret that there's a lot of unhappiness at big law firms, or that this profession is in a crisis with the economy in recession, or that firms exploit and mistreat associates. Many people are angry and frightened and wracked with doubt over their decision to become a lawyer.

It shows strength to show weakness. And there's no shame in admitting you're human.

So break the sacred taboo already and talk about it. Join forces and support one another.

Bring me your stories - post them on the website. Let's have a conversation about what's really going on - and the toll it's taking.

I guarantee you're not alone.

* * *

This column originally ran on March 3, 2010. I was still new to writing for AboveTheLaw, and took the risk here of intentionally appearing to write about a real client. I did so to further the whole point of the column, which was that this client could have been anyone, and that we're all in the same boat. Rest assured, the examples in this piece were nothing more than fictional composites based on bits and pieces of what I see every week. I ran into a lot of flak for it, nonetheless.

No Rest for the Weary

My lawyer clients sometimes arrive at my office complaining about their awful work hours. They talk about how worn out they are, how they pulled all-nighters, came in on weekends, etc.

Other times they come in with a different complaint – there's nothing to do.

Why would that be a problem? Couldn't they relax a bit and catch their breath?

No. Because at law firms, no one is ever supposed to admit there's nothing to do.

Law firms endlessly remind you of their outrageous demands for "billable hours" - but they never so much as whisper that there might not always be sufficient work.

If you've ever attended a partner's meeting, you'll know the rainmakers aren't sitting around gossiping about associates. They're pressuring one another – and especially the young partners – to cultivate clients and drum up business.

One more thing: partners hoard work during dry times. That's why associates feel the drought so severely.

The real issue here isn't that workflow is variable at law firms. It's variable at any business. That's the way the world operates. Of course there will be downtime.

The problem is that this reality isn't acknowledged at law firms. That creates an atmosphere, at least for associates, in which rest, relaxation, a wind-down – whatever you want to call it – is never permitted to happen.

Curiously, downtime does happen elsewhere. When I was in the business world, it was considered a matter of course to grab your coat and head home if things were slow. People respected the work you did, and there was no point in "face time." If things were slow, you took off.

A friend of mine, who worked for years at McKinsey as a consultant, told me they had a phrase for these periods. You were said to be "on the beach" for a few days or weeks. It was acknowledged that this was the case, and no one expected you to do anything but relax and be on call for the next project.

Law firms are different. Here is a culture that abhors rest above all else. You are not supposed to admit you have nothing much to do. There's no work – but the associates cannot enjoy that situation and catch their breath. Instead of resting, you switch from one intense pressure to another – from being exhausted with too much work to being exhausted with worry.

No one admits the situation and says, "Hey, it's slow this week – why don't you take a couple days off?" You are supposed to conjure up something – some matter/client code, no matter how dubious – to bill something to. That's what billing codes like "professional reading" are for. There should be a contest for the most ridiculous euphemism for "sitting around not doing much." I'm sure there are some whoppers out there.

Downtime is important – especially in the American economy, where you already have too little vacation time. Other "semi-recreational" outlets – business lunches, conference weekends, "trainings" and afternoons spent cruising the internet – tend to pick up the slack. Many lawyers feel obligated to spend the slow times sulking guiltily in their offices, avoiding hallways for fear of being spotted looking not-busy. This is bad for everyone's mental health.

You, like everyone else, need a bit of conscious regression sometimes – to let yourself play, and allow your mind to wander. Otherwise, feelings of deprivation can build up and lead to anxiety and depression.

"Regression in the service of the ego," as the psychoanalyst Ernst Kris termed taking a little downtime, might mean heading down to the gym, or savoring a long lunch with a colleague or friend. It might even mean – gasp! – leaving early and catching dinner and a movie, or taking a half-day to hit a museum, without feeling like you're doing something wrong.

Sometimes it's the simple things that make the difference - like enjoying your weekend and taking it for granted your phone won't ring.

Lawyers need to support one another's right to rest. When I was at Sullivan & Cromwell, I witnessed plenty of lunch-room braggadocio about how many thousands of billable hours everyone racked up. It would have been nice, for a change, to hear someone talking about a dinner they'd enjoyed with their family, or a cultural event they'd attended, or a good book they'd found time to read.

There is more to life than work work work.

There's play. You need to rest sometimes. Everyone does.

Originally published April 14, 2010.

Popping Pills at the Office

There was an article in the New York Times a few weeks ago with enormous potential ramifications for lawyers bent over their desks at big law firms. The tentative conclusion of the piece was simple: if you are dealing with minor depression, or in fact, with anything other than serious, major depression, popping anti-depressant pills is probably a waste of time. In fact, a placebo might do you more good.

How many lawyers are currently taking anti-depressants? According to admittedly anecdotal evidence from the lawyers I've seen over the years in my private practice, quite a few.

It's such a lawyerly thing to do. You figure out you're depressed, so you do something about it - march over to your doctor, or maybe a high-powered shrink with a top reputation, get diagnosed, and get your pills. The whole thing takes a few minutes, and you're back on the job. No wasting billable hours, no whining and complaining on a therapist's couch – you take care of the issue and move on. Take a pill and knock it off with the martyr routine.

The problem is anti-depressants come with their own issues...

First, like I said, they might not work. Don't believe me? Here's an excerpt from the article:

Some widely prescribed drugs for depression provide relief in extreme cases but are no more effective than placebo pills for most patients, according to a new analysis released Tuesday. The findings could help settle a longstanding debate about antidepressants. While the study does not imply that the drugs are worthless for anyone with moderate to serious depression — many such people do seem to benefit — it does provide one likely explanation for the sharp disagreement among experts about the drugs' overall effectiveness.

Second, the side-effects. This includes the "sexual side-effects" - which could mean, if you're a guy, erectile dysfunction, and whichever gender you are, inability to reach orgasm. And there are "regular" side effects, too - like weight gain.

Third, anti-depressants only work while you're on them. I've heard of people staying on anti-depressants for decades, but I have no idea what the long-term effects are because no one knows. If you'd like to experiment on yourself, I'm sure the pharmaceutical industry would be fascinated to see what happens.

Fourth, to the extent they do work, it's by erasing feelings. Anti-depressants tend to narrow the bandwidth of what you feel, chopping off the top and the bottom – no more highs, no more lows. That can bring relief, but at a cost.

Fifth, other than the vague explanation that they "affect neurotransmitter levels," no one really understands how they work. Anti-depressant medications, especially the new generation of drugs, are a relatively recent development, and the exact mechanism that produces the results isn't well understood.

Is there another option? Yes – talk therapy.

Some lawyers are skeptics when it comes to psychotherapists.

I'll quote from a comment on AboveTheLaw.com from one of my earlier posts:

This guy [The People's Therapist] gives me even more reason to think that therapists are disgusting creepy slime balls. They think that they somehow have this unbelievable god-like ability to get inside your mind and make everything all better. They have all the answers, if you'll just let them in.

Gross. These people are god-complex freaks. Would never go to a therapist, ever.

Well...okay. A good therapist should welcome authentic thoughts and feelings. And maybe this writer's got a point. Even if pills aren't the answer - why would anyone want to visit a slime ball like me?

The short answer is – while no psychotherapist has a god-like ability to get inside your mind – if he's properly trained, he will know what he's doing, and he can help. Psychotherapy is an effective treatment, especially for depression.

Depression is caused by bottled anger. If you are a depressed client, a psychotherapist will use interventions with you designed to encourage you to talk, and keep talking, in a way that expresses that bottled anger. Before long – I guarantee it – you'll see affect restored, and a more authentic, happier self emerge. Just feeling a right to express the emotions you didn't realize you were holding inside can have a strong healing effect.

It's not a pill, like in Alice in Wonderland or The Matrix. But therapy doesn't have to take forever, and you'll probably feel better after the first session.

So maybe you should ask yourself why you're so distrustful of someone whose job is to listen to you and actually hear what you're saying. Would that really be so bad?

Maybe no one's ever done it before – so you don't trust anyone ever could. That's understandable. It's something you could work on in therapy.

Originally published March 10, 2010.

All That and Then Some...

To judge by the accoutrements of "the profession," lawyers, as a group, maintain an inflated self-image. They think they're all that.

It's easy to get sucked into this mind-set – especially fresh out of law school. Perhaps, when you're not "thinking like a lawyer," you've spent a few minutes admiring the little "Esq." printed after your name on an envelope from school or a law firm - or from some company in Parsippany trying to sell you a genuine brass pen holder featuring a statue of "blind justice" for only $59.99 with free shipping.

Back when I passed the bar, I was offered the option by New York State to purchase a printed document – "suitable for hanging" - to memorialize the event. I figured what the heck and blew the twenty-five bucks. The "parchment" arrived in a cardboard tube, and it was huge - like a royal proclamation. I felt ridiculous, rolled it back up and stuck it in a closet, where it remains.

It's hard to imagine accountants (who sometimes earn more than lawyers), or bankers (who always earn more than lawyers) laying on the pretension to quite the degree lawyers take for granted.

My father was a physician, and in his early days, he fell for the professional ostentation thing. After he graduated from medical school, he ordered "MD" plates for his car. Sure enough, the next time he took the rusty old Mercury Marquis in for a repair, the mechanics charged him double. That was enough - he sent back the plates.

At least doctors are highly regarded in our society. My father was a psychiatrist, not a brain surgeon, but there was a grudging respect for the fact of his MD. If you were in an accident or had a heart attack on a plane, theoretically my dad could save your life. That meant something.

With lawyers, self-esteem outpaces public acclaim. That's because, for the most part, non-lawyers view lawyers as worthless parasites (or at least, as existing on the worthless, parasitical end of the esteem spectrum.)

I'll never forget the time I asked a Wall Street-er what he actually thought about lawyers.

I'd received the nudge from Sullivan & Cromwell, which meant I had six months to find another job. A head-hunter somehow or other set me up with an interview to be a bond trader at JP Morgan.

I considered the whole idea misguided – I was a lawyer from one of the top firms in the world, and far above working as a mere *trader*. I imagined bond traders as slick goombahs with Staten Island accents shouting into phones all day. I was an *attorney*, with a degree from *Hahvard*. I showed up at Morgan as a *courtesy* to the headhunter. I radiated disdain.

For their part, the traders were patient and polite. I chatted briefly, answered some "brain-teaser" questions, and left. That was that.

During that weekend, by sheer coincidence, I read "Liar's Poker," and learned something about bond traders – specifically, the fact that they earn millions of dollars a year. Somehow, as that information sank in, I began to reconsider my attitude towards this *opportunity*.

Monday morning, I called up my contact at Morgan, the guy who interviewed me. He was Australian, and seemed distantly friendly. For whatever reason, I sensed I had nothing to lose, so I put it to him straight. I'd been reading "Liar's Poker," I said, and sensed I'd blown the interview. I wanted another chance to present myself.

There was a pause.

"I appreciate that mate. It took guts to make this call, and I'll keep you in mind. Unfortunately, someone's taken the job. You did show a typical lawyer attitude - I'm afraid it hurt your chances."

I asked him to explain.

"That's why I tell headhunters not to send me lawyers. You all act like you're too good for the place. I'll never understand it."

I asked, flat out, what he really thought of lawyers.

Another pause, then, delivered in that charming Australian accent, with a chuckle: "Bend over and take it like a man."

"That's really what you think?"

"Seems like the worst job in the world to us. You work day and night, chasing your own tail. You're like slaves, and all you do is the boring stuff."

"Trading bonds is more fun, huh?"

"Fun and lucrative, thank you."

That was the first honest conversation I'd ever had with a non-lawyer about lawyers - and it was an eye-opener. It led me to re-run through my head all the interactions I'd had at closings over the years with the other, non-lawyer participants at the table. The relaxed, friendly guys from the ratings agencies always showed up at the last minute like it was no big deal. The auditors from the big accounting firms smiled all the time, radiating contentment. The bright, perky bankers from Goldman, Sachs looked – well, like someone dropping by their lawyers' office to sign documents, then take off for an early lunch. By comparison, we'd inevitably been up all night in our wool suits, and were sweaty, red-eyed and miserable.

Somehow or other, though... we thought we were hot stuff. Why?

I had a junior partner from a large law firm pose the same question to me in my office the other day. He was remarking in amazement at a senior partner who'd complained things were getting so complex he couldn't trust "the really difficult stuff" to junior partners anymore – he had to do everything himself.

"Can you imagine?" My client said. "This guy was so arrogant he didn't trust his fellow partners. That's the level of ego we're dealing with. He's gotten to where he thinks he's the only person who can do anything right. And between you and me, his writing is terrible – long-winded, pretentious, riddled with hyperbole. He thinks every sentence is a masterpiece. But he's so senior, no one can say anything to him."

Arrogance is a defense against insecurity. And it's insecurity that drives many people to pursue law.

Lawyers often tell me they entered law because they needed to "be somebody" - to achieve status, power, a degree, a title, an office and a secretary. You go from being the guy who graduated from college and doesn't know what he wants to do, to...somebody. You are provided with a defense against the dreaded cocktail party question – so what do you do?

Many lawyers went into law to hide the fact they don't really know what they're good at. All the pretense and pomposity surrounding the profession amounts to an attempt to run from the feeling that they're still a bit of a fake – one of the relatively uninspired, resolutely above-average.

Nobody's fooling anyone.

* * *

This piece was originally published on May 25, 2011. Amazing as it seems, the bulk of the online response to this piece was a lengthy and rancorous debate over whether accountants could really earn as much as lawyers. No one was disputing that bankers leave lawyers in the dust salary-wise – but accountants?! This was too much – an insult not to be borne. From what I could make out in the flurry of back and forth, accountants have a longer partnership path – but the law partnership path is lengthening too, and it's a major long shot. Once you've made partner, accountants at the big firms also seem to earn more. Accountants have a lower starting salary – but they don't have the crippling school loans or the massive over-supply that creates high unemployment among lawyers. You could debate this issue forever, but at the end of the day, my take on things seems correct: accountants often earn more than lawyers. They might have more fun, too. The bigger issue is simple: law is a lousy profession to choose if you're only choosing it for money and status. You might be better off getting a CPA – or following your heart and doing something you enjoy.

When the Emptiness
Swallows You Whole

Last October, an ex-lawyer friend of mine forwarded me an email with a juicy piece of Biglaw gossip: A former associate at Sullivan & Cromwell had offed himself. He was thirty-nine. The body was discovered beneath a highway bridge in Toronto. A few days earlier, it was revealed that since the mid-90's, he and a co-conspirator had pocketed ten million dollars through an insider trading scheme. He'd stolen confidential information from S&C, arriving early in the morning to dig through waste baskets, rifle partners' desks and employ temporary word-processor codes to break into the computer system. He shared this information with his co-conspirator, who used it for insider trading, then split the profits.

"You can't make this shit up," was my friend's comment. "Wasn't he from around your time?"

It took a minute to locate the face. Gil Cornblum. Jewish (like me), a bit pudgy, with round glasses. Gil, in that ridiculous little office two doors down from mine.

What was Gil like? Mild-mannered, pleasant, always smiling. I should have known something was wrong.

The pieces fit together. Gil kept weird hours. He used to chuckle that he liked to get in early so he didn't have to stay late. It turned out he was getting in at 5 am, combing the firm for insider data.

There was a lavish wedding, too. A mutual friend was invited up to Canada to watch Gil tie the knot, and was blown away by the display. He'd never imagined Gil had that kind of money.

As people do in these situations, I stopped for a moment to contemplate Gil's death. His body was discovered at the bottom of a highway bridge. He was still breathing, according to the bits of news I found online.

So far as I can tell, that means portly, lovable Gil Cornblum threw himself off a bridge on a Canadian highway in the middle of the night and lay on the bottom – of what? A rocky riverbed? - shattered and dying.

Suicide amounts to punishing whoever is supposed to take care of you because you feel their care is inadequate. You are angry, so you destroy the thing they love, or were supposed to love – you.

Certainly, the care we all received at S&C was inadequate, and we committed suicide a little each day just by staying there and putting ourselves through that abuse as our lives passed us by. Our slow suicide manifested in other ways as well. Most of us mistreated ourselves by neglecting our health, letting our friendships die off, ignoring our families, our hobbies, our lives. There was a cry for help in all that self-neglect, a cry of victimhood – it said "Look how many hours I work! Look how little I have left for myself!" and finally, implicitly "Look how little care I receive! Look how I'm falling apart as a result!" We were all broadcasting – or most of us were – on all frequencies, the same message – misery, unhappiness, neglect. We were all crying for help.

Maybe insider trading was Gil's grand, angry gesture of protest against the abuse he received. He put his entire life on the line, knowing he might well be caught, end up in jail and lose everything. He was playing Russian roulette, and maybe he knew he'd kill himself if he got caught.

And all for what? Money. In psychotherapy, money is a surrogate for care, for security in love. We all felt insecure and unloved at S&C – we knew we could be fired any day, and rarely heard so much as a kind word directed our way. Maybe insider trading and stolen money gave Gil a counter-balance. Maybe it was meant to compensate for everything else missing in that pointless existence. They stole much that was valuable from him – and he stole right back from them in return.

Were the rest of us so different? Weren't we all trading our lives for money? No one would have worked in that hellhole if they hadn't waved six-figure salaries in our faces.

The high suicide rate among lawyers isn't hard to explain: you trade away your life for money and clutch at possessions to substitute for what's missing. You're already dying.

When it doesn't work, and money fails to answer your needs, the rage overflows. You punish the world for denying you the care you crave.

End result? The ultimate victory through defeat. You take your own life.

Discharging unconscious anger feels good. It's a primitive, simple pleasure. It's also incredibly destructive. Gil – who came across as a mild-mannered, pleasant Canadian – was probably high as a kite on the rage he discharged by stealing millions of dollars right under those partners' noses.

His rage consumed the money and kept going. It finally consumed his life.

I remember Gil Cornblum as a nice guy. I can't find it in me to come down on him too harshly for his crimes. I suppose he felt he had to steal that money, to compensate for working at a place as miserable as S&C. He was trying to fill an emptiness that, to some degree, we all sensed around us.

Goodbye, Gil.

I'm sorry the emptiness finally opened wide enough to swallow you whole.

* * *

This was one of my first pieces for AboveTheLaw - it originally ran on February 16, 2010. I received a lot of comments in response. Some people seemed to miss the point – they wanted to convince me Gil was a bad person – or at least that he'd done bad things. I don't necessarily equate the two. Gil was a nice person, who made mistakes, and paid a high price – a tragic price – for those mistakes. I continue to remember him fondly as one of the few bright spots during my time at S&C.

Your Dark Lord

I was chuckling with a client the other day about the insanity of trying to please a partner with a piece of written work. The trick, she said – and I've heard this before – is to adopt the voice of the partner. That's what he wants – something that sounds like him. It doesn't matter if your style is better than his. He wants to hear himself.

My client can imitate the writing styles of five partners. That includes whatever quirks - run-on sentences, rudeness, biting sarcasm, unnecessary adjectives, circuitous explanations – capture that partner's unique gift. It's a piece of cake: assemble substance, add ventriloquy, and voila! - a happy partner.

She learned this trick after receiving mark-ups. Her heart would sink as she combed the scribble for a critical error. But there was never anything there – only her failure to clone.

This is an example of a more generalized phenomenon - partners, as a group, tend to be arrogant and narcissistic. They harbor absurd notions about their own abilities and tend not to notice anyone else's right to exist.

Nothing new. But it's interesting to ask why.

Law firms are abattoirs of self-esteem. If you think you might be a good, useful, capable person, give yourself a few weeks in the world of Biglaw and you'll come to realize you have no ability whatsoever, are in way over your head and were a fool to consider you might succeed at anything.

That's the special magic of a law firm.

You are also entirely alone. Everyone else is flourishing. They're doing fine. It's only you. You are the problem.

How do they achieve this feat of psychic disassembly?

For starters, nary a kind word.

If you put dozens of pleasers in the same room, everyone tries to please everyone else. No one acknowledges he's pleased. That's not what pleasers do.

Everyone can't try to impress. Someone has to *be* impressed. That person would do the hard work of thanking and praising the others – "You're doing a great job. I appreciate your effort."

You'll never hear that sort of piffle at a law firm. In a world where everyone is starved for praise, no one has time to waste feeding anyone else's confidence.

Two defenses, arrogance and narcissism, permit lawyers to survive in this hostile environment.

The simplest defense against self-doubt is arrogance. Inside you're scared, so you pump yourself up for others to see.

The simplest defense against isolation is narcissism. You're afraid no one wants to be with you, so you tune them out.

Arrogance always appears a bit comical because it's so obvious. If you're terrified you might not have what it takes, you put on a false bravado, but it doesn't fool anyone. And once you've taken the leap into arrogance, you're stuck - you have to maintain it, or risk humiliation.

Narcissism is more insidious, and less amusing. If you're not receiving anything you need from anyone else, you shut them out – put up a mirror – and stare at a world that looks like you.

Maybe you must be an arrogant narcissist to make partner. That would certainly explain some things.

The downside is that you become an arrogant narcissist. The money's good – but no one can stand you. You wind up correcting memos to sound like you wrote them. You don't realize you're doing it.

J.K. Rowling, in her Harry Potter series, presents a flawless portrait of a Biglaw partner.

Lord Voldemort is an arrogant narcissist to the core. When The

Dark Lord (as he's known) arranges for a Death Eater associate to pen a memorandum, there's no doubt he wants it to sound like something he wrote. And you can rest assured he's not going to be Mr.-Supportive-of-Your-Feelings if it doesn't.

He-Who-Must-Not-Be-Named fears death because it challenges the reality of his omnipotence - the total control he wields over others' lives. To guard against that eventuality, Voldemort employs black magic, shattering his soul into splinters which he secretes away in the form of small, magical items known as horcruxes. If you find one of these evil items, you must destroy it. Otherwise Voldemort and his insidious power will never die.

To wear the horcrux is to bear the weight of the Dark Lord's wicked soul. He is with you through the horcrux, and his power threatens to overwhelm your spirit.

A partner at a law firm doesn't call the evil splinter of his shattered soul a horcrux.

He calls it a Blackberry - the container of his arrogant narcissism.

To carry this cursed object is to bear a weight of pure malignancy.

A partner cannot die until each Blackberry is destroyed. Only then can you free yourself of his evil.

When an innocent junior first approaches the dark force of a partner, the arrogant narcissism might overwhelm, or even kill. You've seen juniors who mysteriously disappear in the first month. But on occasion, the spell is deflected, and the associate himself becomes a horcrux, a container for a fragment of the partner's twisted passions. A link joins them, and he haunts the associate's dreams like a terrible memory returned to life.

In trying to obliterate your mortal soul, the partner kills a part of himself. The evil within you must be destroyed before it metastasizes into the cancer of arrogant narcissism.

Don't let him doom you to his own wretched fate.

You could make partner.

Originally published January 19, 2011.

A Little "Me Time"

My client wasn't getting enough sleep. I assumed it was insomnia, but that didn't fit the bill. It wasn't that she *couldn't* sleep – it was that she *wouldn't* sleep. She was staying up from 11 pm to 2 am, lying in bed mostly, playing Angry Birds.

Those few hours were the only time she was left alone all day – no one from the firm called to assign her something awful to do or yell at her for something awful she'd done. To relinquish this sliver of "me time" – even for sleep – was out of the question.

Morning to night, she spent at the firm. Weekends didn't exist, in any meaningful sense – they were workdays. Laundry went undone, as did other stuff, like getting her driver's license renewed or her taxes filed. The only hours devoted to anything for herself were stolen from her sleep schedule, and spent slingshotting daredevil birds at sneering pigs (that's an Angry Birds reference.)

She needed to vegetate. You need to vegetate, too. There's only so much work anyone can do. That's why you find yourself playing video games at 2 am instead of sleeping. You need to play and you need to sleep. You need both.

A medical resident told me law sounded worse than medicine. At least with medicine when you're on-call, you're on-call, and when you're not, you're not. With law, you're always on call. Just because you're asleep in bed doesn't mean you shouldn't be working.

Another lawyer client crawled home from the office recently after midnight, only to be awakened at 3 am by the alarm on her Blackberry. She

93

turned it off, then noticed an email from a senior associate, still at his desk. She glanced at the email, but decided to ignore it – nothing critical - and deal with him in the morning.

She forgot his account was set up so he could see she'd opened the email.

Her Blackberry buzzed through the night, with increasingly desperate messages. "What happened? I know you read my email. Why aren't you responding?!"

The last one arrived at 5:30 am.

Law firms operate on the assumption they own your soul. There's no downtime. They own your soul on Christmas morning. They own your soul at 5 am. They own your soul when you're on vacation. They own your soul when you're in the hospital. There is no "me time."

That doesn't work, because you need "me time." Thus, there is an apparent contradiction. So you find a work-around – what we contract attorneys call a "carve-out" - an exception. And that exception becomes your "me time."

The all-time favorite work-around is to get liquored up and sloppy. If you're drunk... well, there's your carve out: they can come a-callin', but you're not gonna go a-lawyerin', now are you? Voila! "Me time."

Problem is, as a lawyer, you can't go completely wild, at least, not on a school night (which is pretty much every night). So you arrive at the concept of maintenance drinking.

Lawyers appear at my office sometimes looking suspiciously okay. On occasion, I think I've stumbled on that mythical beast – the happy lawyer. And at a big firm, too! Then he mentions the four whiskies he gulps down every single night before going to bed. Oh, and the eight or ten (or twelve) drinks he downs if he doesn't have to go into the office the next day.

He looks fine at the firm. Might not be loving it, but he's surviving. He's put in five or six years - might even go for partner. Nothing looks wrong, unless you're there for an hour around 11 pm when he downs half a bottle of Maker's Mark.

Time spent getting drunk can be "me time." It's escape, in the form of substance abuse. It's also an outlet for anger. People in the recovery movement talk about "drinking on anger." If you're abusing alcohol, you're always drinking on anger. It's aggressive, doing something you know is bad for you - and something that will remove you from the world. It's not just checking out and saying I'm not here. It's saying "fuck you."

Getting stoned every night isn't much different. Pot is less physically addictive and easier on your body than booze, but doing constant bong hits is tuning out the world, and tuning out yourself – and that's an aggressive statement. It says "fuck you" and it says "this is my only escape – I've run out of other options." Let me be clear: I've met many lawyers in prestigious jobs who go home and get high each and every night. Smoking weed once in a while – like having a drink once in a while – is one thing. Maintenance smoking – and drinking – is another thing entirely.

Coming home and yelling at your husband or wife is yet another option for "me time" – that's the rage-a-holic's drug of choice. You get home late every night from the firm, and your wife looks forward to spending a few pleasant hours alone together. Instead, you turn into a beast, slamming doors and tearing into her for anything and everything.

The rage-a-holic's "me time" is about ruining the other person's "us time." I've heard lawyers tell me they can't control it – you need to get the anger out of your system. The endless constriction of life in Biglaw feels like a cage. One client had a dream he was trapped in a concrete chair - he couldn't sit up, couldn't budge. That's how if feels, slaving for years to pay off a bank, while a control-freak partner dictates every hour of your day.

Rage is helpless anger. Impulsively, you address it by discharging aggression, which is gratifying, at least in the short term. It feels good to terrorize someone helpless – until later, when the hang-over comes, and awareness of the hurt you've caused, and possibly the end of your relationship, the one meaningful thing you have left.

During my Sullivan & Cromwell years, my "me time" was mostly spent with my dog. My boyfriend was away at architecture grad school, so I hardly saw him. The timing seemed perfect – I was stuck at a firm, and he was buried in design charrettes. My companion, always delighted to see me, was Margaret, a skye terrier.

She had a dog-walker, but that was hardly enough. I saw the look in Margaret's eyes when I crawled home late at night, only to disappear back to the office an hour later. Dogs need a little "me time," too.

There is no such thing as work/life balance when you're a slave to the billable hour. That reality takes a toll on your psyche. You require time that's truly yours – not a tantrum of acting out before you fall asleep.

One client told me her plan for a future legal career:

Take a clerkship,
work briefly at firm,
leave for second clerkship,
work briefly at firm,
get pregnant
take maternity leave
get pregnant again
take maternity leave
take accumulated vacation time
refuse (subtly) to work
get fired
receive unemployment.

This scheme sounds exploitative, but it has an undeniable logic – at least she's factored in plenty of "me time."

Firms don't hesitate to look after their own interests. I've heard stories of new hires being deferred for a year without warning, or half a class of associates getting laid off after four months.

Apparently big law firms need a little "me time" – some space for themselves, to put their priorities first.

So do you.

Originally published June 8, 2011.

You're in Trouble

Remember when you were a kid, and you got caught doing something you shouldn't, and a big cloud formed over your head?

You were "in trouble."

The other kids sort of inched out of your path and exchanged looks. They didn't want any piece of what you had coming. Mom was going to talk to you later. Or dad. You'd done something wrong.

It feels that way sometimes at a big law firm - in fact, a lot of the time.

Maybe you forget to ask a crucial question during a deposition. Or you wrote a memo that didn't have the answer your partner wanted. Maybe – and this happened to me once - you ended up getting berated for being "too friendly" to the other side at a drafting conference. Maybe you're still not sure exactly what you did wrong, but it must have been something. It's always something.

The cloud hangs over you in the office and follows you home. When you were a kid, it eventually dissipated, but now it lingers indefinitely. What's really going on?

A little dose of anxiety is being injected into you, in the form of a thought.

Anxiety is triggered by cognition – predictive thoughts. You predict something bad is going to happen, so you clutch up in preparation – tense up and prepare for attack.

At a law firm, the standard predictive cognition – the expectation - is that you are going to be criticized. They do that a lot at law firms. It is a fair guess that if something goes wrong, you are going to be blamed – and things go wrong all the time.

It got to the point for me, at Sullivan & Cromwell, that I felt my entire body clench in preparation for attack just walking through the doors of 125 Broad Street and stepping into that elevator.

When you spend long periods of time tensed up, on alert for attack, it takes a toll on your nervous system. In fact, it can produce lasting damage.

In World War I, soldiers spent weeks in trenches under fire, crouched in terror, waiting for that next bomb or bullet with their name on it. Those were some of the first documented cases of what was called "shell shock" then and is now referred to as PTSD – Post-Traumatic Stress Disorder.

It might seem a stretch to suggest that lawyers at big law firms suffer from PTSD symptoms.

But that's exactly what I'm doing.

PTSD has three general "clusters" of symptoms:
- hyper-arousal (an "on guard" or "easily startled" feeling)
- numbing/avoidance (emotional deadening)
- intrusive (flashbacks, nightmares)

I've worked with lawyers who are literally jumpy from the sense of having enemies – hyper-critical, angry attacking partners – spring out at them whenever they let down their guard.

I've seen lawyers who have numbed themselves until they barely admit to feeling emotions, even in a therapist's office.

And yes, lawyers have nightmares about their firms. One former attorney had a recurrent dream in which he realized he was back in his old office. He knew the dream so well he'd start thinking his way out of it right from the start, reassuring himself it wasn't like it used to be – that he'd left the firm, they didn't own him, they couldn't hurt him anymore, he could grab his coat and walk out the door.

Some law firm environments are so punishing and toxic they produce trauma and trigger PTSD symptoms. At least, that's what I've witnessed over the years from lawyers I've seen as clients.

My best advice for anyone working under these conditions is to get some support - and to leave this environment as soon as possible.

At very least, you need to create a "safe zone" - or multiple "safe zones" where you can let down your guard and relax. That might mean finding an hour in your day to hit the gym, or take a yoga class. It might mean walking through the park during lunch, or eating outside and watching children in the playground. It might mean setting aside time to spend with good friends, no matter how busy you are. It might mean making sure you disappear into a book, or your favorite video game, for half an hour before you go to sleep at night. The key is reserving a bit of time when you can feel safe, secure, and intact within yourself. And yes, it might mean taking an hour each week to talk to a therapist – visiting a place where the focus is on you and there are no distractions.

You can't spend your life "in trouble." The price you pay for living under a cloud might be higher than you think.

* * *

This piece ran on March 17, 2010, and drew a lot of flak. Some readers attacked me for suggesting you could suffer from PTSD merely from working at a law firm. But that's not what I said. My claim is that you can acquire symptoms of PTSD from working at a law firm. I don't care to get into an argument over the precise criteria for a PTSD diagnosis according to the Diagnostic and Statistical Manual. My point is that working at a law firm can be bad for your mental health - and I've worked with people who show signs of trauma from their experiences in these environments. I stand by that claim.

Splitting Hairs

An editor at AboveTheLaw suggested some months back I do a piece on the US News & World Report law school rankings. For whatever reason, this decrepit old news weekly - which someone must still read - has created a sideline publishing rankings of schools, including law schools. I'm not sure what the criteria are, but at least in theory, it's a big deal for lawyers when the list comes out each year.

The rankings seem designed to make official what everyone knows anyway, i.e., that there are "prestige" schools that are harder to get into. But like any good opinion piece, they throw in a few twists - familiar names in unexpected places. It boils down to dissing one of the big places, or unexpectedly anointing a second-rank outfit. That way everyone can get riled up over the respective rankings of my school versus your school.

It sounded kind of boring, so I filed the idea away.

Then it started to gnaw at me. The US News list seemed like a good example of the amazing lengths lawyers go to in order to distinguish themselves from other lawyers. The problem is that the career path is so conservative. For years, every lawyer does pretty much the same exact thing, beginning with lining up to take the LSAT. Then you get processed and distributed to law schools based on hairline distinctions. In class you sit through identical lectures, take identical exams, and head off – for the most part – to identical firms to do nearly identical work.

You end up arguing over the details – splitting hairs.

The law school curriculum, for example, is the same wherever you go - I doubt the property law lecture at a "top" law school is much different, let alone superior, to a property law lecture at a less "prestigious" place. But, of course the students are "better" at the more prestigious school – because they did better on their LSAT. How much better? Some tiny fraction of a percentage, probably, representing a few questions that they got right and someone else got wrong.

I worked with one lawyer who went to a "second-tier" law school in New York, but rose to the top of his class and made law review. He said he still faces resistance at top firms because of snobbery over where he went to school – even though he's been out and working for eight years. Those Yale and Harvard lawyers at the big firms, he says, turn their noses up at his top-of-the-class record at a "lesser" school – as well as his federal clerkship and the years of hard work that followed.

I'm currently working with a couple of young lawyers who find themselves in the odd position of trying to decide how to appraise the value of a "top school." One woman was accepted at a top place, but offered a full scholarship at a "second-tier" institution. Is it worth $170k to go to the prestige school? The education itself will be nearly identical. Is the snob value worth it? According to one of my clients, half the kids at Columbia Law are struggling to find jobs right now, so it doesn't sound like the top places are pulling their weight. On the other hand, maybe it's even worse coming out of a second-tier joint. Crucially, though - with no debt, she wouldn't be as desperate as everyone else. I see plenty of young lawyers emerging from top schools (and every other kind of school) with shaky job prospects, huge debt and – worst of all – the sense that going into law was a mistake. Their school debt reduces them to indentured servitude, making it impossible to do anything but law, at least until they've paid the piper.

How about the law firms themselves? Surely some are "better" than others?

I remember, during my first summer of law school, when I was interning at the ACLU, one of the staff attorneys sat me down with another intern to make a list of the top New York City firms, and explain the "facts of life." Essentially, he ranked the firms into three tiers – top, middle and bottom. That was probably splitting hairs already. Many of those firms were essentially identical. But I dutifully memorized the list.

Later, when I got to the interview process, the firms all asked me why I was choosing their firm in particular. I rattled on with the standard answers about atmosphere, culture, practice areas, and so forth, but I was making it all up. I had no idea what I was talking about. How could I? I was a law student. In the end, I chose the most "prestigious" place I could, based on that guy's list.

In fact, most of those firms were interchangeable. Sure, you might work with one person instead of another, and that could make a difference. But once the grind set in, the attorneys I worked with at two different firms began to seem interchangeable. The practice area distinction didn't even make much difference as a junior associate – it was just work.

I had a corporations professor at NYU who was a partner at Wachtell. He mused once during a lecture on whether "corporate lawyers are essentially fungible." To my surprise, his answer was uncertain - he admitted they might be.

Does that surprise and outrage you? Would you be as upset if he'd suggested accountants or dentists were fungible? To some degree, even doctors are fungible, or ought to be, right? They should be able to do their jobs, and if you need your appendix removed, anyone who calls himself a general surgeon ought to be able to do a decent job removing it.

It could be the fear of "fungibility" that produces the harsh, hyper-critical atmosphere at so many law firms. Everyone's a critic because they're all afraid they might be more or less just like everyone else.

I took it for granted at Sullivan & Cromwell that the senior associates would treat me like something under their shoe, but it always surprised me when another junior associate would put me down in front of a senior, or obviously compete to prove he was "better" than me at my job. I suppose he wanted to make partner, and that meant proving that his mindless, endless grind of work was superior to my mindless, endless grind of work.

Now that I'm working with partners as clients, it amazes me to hear the competition never stops. One partner at a big firm told me he felt more beat up after making partner than before, because once he'd made it to the big-time, the gloves came off. His fellow partners competed viciously to prove they were the ones bringing in business – and had a claim to the biggest slice of the partnership pie.

Perhaps if everyone in law were enjoying themselves more – savoring the work and finding satisfaction in the field, they wouldn't have to concentrate so much on drawing distinctions where none exist. They could get on with what they're doing, support and praise one another's work - and stop paying attention to nonsense like the US News & World Report law school rankings.

* * *

This piece was originally published on June 30, 2010, to coincide with the release of the US News & World Report law school rankings – or at least, I think it was, since I'm still not sure when they come out. It was an editor's idea. My goal was to express how little I care about law school rankings. Mission accomplished, I hope.

A Little Chat

Some big law firms are like the mob. They do ugly things, but prefer to avoid "ugliness." The partners, like the capos of major crime families, have delicate constitutions.

Ugliness could result from ill-considered communication. For that reason, a capo – or a partner - isn't going to tell you what he really thinks. That would be *indelicate*. It could lead to *misunderstandings*.

You, in turn, shouldn't tell a partner what you really think. That could lead to *sleeping with the fishes*.

My client recently received a lesson in partner communication.

The firm was slow, and she was dedicating her time to a big pro bono case, which was the most meaningful thing she had on her plate. An email suddenly arrived announcing a new policy: you now needed special permission to bill over 250 pro bono hours annually. In two months, she'd billed 220, and the case might be coming to trial.

She called the pro bono partner.

"You're close to the limit," he noted.

Last week, there was no limit, she explained. This is an important case.

"You've nearly exceeded the cap on hours," he helpfully re-noted.

She inhaled deeply, and re-explained the situation. He was clearly implying that he wanted her to back off, let someone else take over, let the case slide. She didn't want to do that, but he wasn't going to back down.

He ingeniously pointed out that the 250 hours cap was the firm's new policy...

...at which point she snapped, and did the unthinkable: she *said what she really thought.*

"I didn't *know* there was a new policy. No one *communicates* at this place. And what is the *point* of this crap? I'm right in the middle of this case. It doesn't even make sense!"

There was a lengthy pause.

"I'm sorry to hear that," said the partner.

He hung up - and she began to harbor second thoughts.

I'm sorry to hear that.

Behold, a singularly dreaded phrase. It is not good news, at a law firm, when you hear "I'm sorry to hear that."

Generally speaking, when you hear "I'm sorry to hear that," at a law firm, it means "you will soon be fired."

There is something worse you could hear – worse than "I'm sorry to hear that."

There's *"I think we should talk about..."*

At a law firm, when you hear "I think we should talk about..." you've already been fired.

Partners don't toss around "I'm sorry to hear that" in casual conversation. It is reserved for serious situations. If a major earthquake strikes, and the floors of the firm pancake, squashing attorneys into paste, it would likely trigger "I'm sorry to hear that..." It could escalate all the way to "I think we should talk about..."

For the most part, "I think we should talk about" is reserved for the single most crucial conversation in the entire law firm conversational repertoire, the *ne plus ultra* of conversations - to wit: *"I think we should talk about your billable hours."*

This exchange, undertaken under secrecy at the highest levels of power, plays out something like this:

"*I think we should talk about your billable hours.*"

"Well, it has been slow. Work doesn't seem to be coming in."

"*I'm sorry to hear that.*"

This conversation, which fuses the twin forces of "I think we should talk about" and "I'm sorry to hear that" into one redoubtable *melange*, roughly parallels the situation of being called into Don Corleone's office – well, let's say tied up, stuffed into the trunk of a Chrysler, and delivered to his office - for *a little chat*.

The Don gazes at you with tender concern, then shakes his head sadly.

"*I think we should talk about* the fact that the money from the First National Bank job has been...*misplaced*."

"Honestly, Godfather, I have no idea. I promise you – I swear on my mother's life – I didn't take the money. I don't know where it is. I would never steal from the family. I swear to God..."

"*I'm sorry to hear that.*"

At this point in time, it's fair to say, your days are numbered.

Same thing at a law firm. On one single occasion during my entire tenure at Sullivan & Cromwell, I encountered "*I think we should talk about...*" That's all it took.

It was delivered to me by the partner in charge of associates. He'd already fired me, gently – or, at least, I think that's what he did. At my review, there was mention of some *ugliness* with an of-counsel who questioned my *commitment* to our work together. The partner was *sorry to hear that*. It was suggested I might find myself *somewhere else* within, say, six months.

Six months later, to the day, I received a call from that same partner.

"*I think we should talk about...*"

Twelve years have passed since that call. I remain profoundly grateful for a job offer I received – in a non-legal position – the day before.

I didn't need to wake up next to a horse's head.

He'd made himself *understood*.

Originally published May 11, 2011.

Not a Baby Bird

I received this letter recently. Yes, it's real, but I've removed anything identifiable to protect the sender:

Hi Will,

I read your thoughts of the legal profession on Above the Law and thought you neatly summarized my situation. I wish I was the type of person who could expel all the anger but instead I feel my self esteem disintegrating. It's starting to become apparent to my co-workers (i.e. I cry at work). There's one other female associate in my office and she's going through the same thing. My problem is I believe the negative things my bosses tell me. I explained this to my boss (when he asked why we were crying) and promised him I would try to develop better coping skills. How do I make myself not care when he goes off on me?

For better or worse, this letter is typical – I hear a lot of stories like this.

A psychotherapist I used to work with – a grizzled veteran of the therapy trenches – used to tell clients he wished he could make the world a better place, but he couldn't. He could only better prepare them to deal with the world the way it is.

That's how I feel about law firms. They can be brutal, and I can't do much about that. But there are ways to deal.

My advice to this woman is to stop acting like a baby bird.

Allow me to explain.

Under stress, it is natural to regress to a child-like way of relating to the world. That's because stress makes you feel overwhelmed, which is how young children, who are small and helpless, feel all the time. Feeling small, helpless and overwhelmed takes you back to a time early in your life, and old behaviors kick in. You can start relating to authority figures like parent figures, focusing on pleasing them and forgetting that you have an adult's right to judge your own behavior on your own terms - to fight back and defend yourself.

There's a good evolutionary reason why children are such natural parent-pleasers. A child evolves *to survive* by pleasing a parent. That's because nature can be brutal – and so can parents. It has been demonstrated again and again that, lacking sufficient food, a mother bird will toss a new-born chick out of the nest to die. It happens in most species. At some level, the parent animal is selecting the child who *fails to please* for culling.

Baby chicks are warm and fuzzy. Nature is not. When a little bird fails to please its parent, that chick quite rightly panics and blames herself – and frantically tries to please as though her life depends on it - which, in fact, it might.

You don't have to act like a baby chick. Not at a law firm.

If you fail to please a partner, you don't have to panic like a child and locate the blame within yourself. That will only cause your self-esteem to plummet and regress you all the way back to a weeping infant.

That path leads directly to depression.

Awareness of what you're doing could be enough to snap you out of it. You're not a child – and that miserable partner isn't your dad. You're an adult, and you're doing your best. You might not always be right – but you probably aren't always wrong, either. Meanwhile, he sounds like a jerk who doesn't know how to manage.

Managing means motivating and inspiring an employee. It means finding a way to praise work, and keeping the feedback constructive and upbeat, so your employee always has an attainable goal – a way to do better. That's what it means to motivate.

Some of you might be ready to write in and say I'm being too soft – that this lawyer is probably doing a bad job and deserves criticism. But even if that were true – and I see no reason to assume it is - this guy still appears to be a terrible manager. You don't make people cry. Not at the office. That isn't motivating.

You might also claim this associate is being manipulative and using tears as a way to control her boss. To some degree, that's probably true. From the sound of things, the partner is abusing his position – and the associate is being inappropriate as well by regressing to a degree that is distracting and unprofessional.

There isn't much I can do about that partner who is a poor manager. But if you find yourself in this associate's position, there are better ways to handle this kind of person. For starters, you can snap out of the regression, and act like an adult. This is not an appropriate situation in which to break down in tears. It is a situation in which you could own your right to anger, and take action to help yourself.

You're not helpless. You are capable of objectively critiquing your own work, and knowing how you're doing. For most associates at law firms, the problem is that you know, objectively, you're doing good work, or at least trying your best – but you're not receiving the recognition you deserve. That's typical. The trick is to stop expecting water from a dry well. Law firms are filled with terrible managers who never praise employees. You have to understand and accept that as a fact of life. You may have to be your own boss to some degree - objectively critique yourself and remind yourself of past achievements - in order to maintain a realistic view of your accomplishments and abilities. That, sadly, is part of working at a law firm.

You could also stop breaking down emotionally during confrontations with lousy managers. Instead, you could take a time-out to pull yourself together, and speak to a partner like this one about his people skills - and maybe get a job with someone less socially autistic.

Fight back. Let that partner push you out of the nest. You're not a baby bird. You'll do just fine on your own.

Originally published June 1, 2010.

The Provider

Every guy with a family feels the urge to pack a bag, get in the car and drive. At least, sometimes.

A client told me that – a straight guy with kids. I don't think it's a straight thing, though. It might not be a guy thing, either. It can be a lawyer thing. Any lawyer with loans experiences the impulse to hit the highway. When you're "The Provider," you do constant battle with the itch to hightail it out of town.

Who's "The Provider"?

It's someone you morph into. A character from an Updike novel...or maybe it's Cheever. Maybe it's Mad Men. You become a cliché from 1950's or early 60's tv shows: Dad, who arrives home, pecks the wife on the cheek, tousles the kids' hair, then collapses into a La-Z-Boy and reads the paper while the golden retriever fetches your bedroom slippers.

...except it sucks bad enough that you're feeling the urge to pack a bag, get in the car and drive.

I'm not saying getting married and having kids is terrible. That's how you got into this mess – you want the wife and the kids. As one of my clients bemoaned, "I want to be a good father. I want to be a good husband. I just can't pull it off with this job, and it's killing me."

The problem is trying to be a lawyer and The Provider at the same time. That's the part that doesn't work.

The basic principle, when you're The Provider, is simple: you pay for everything. This has a certain seductive quality. Many lawyers get into this work because they want to be The Provider. Maybe your father didn't earn much, and mom had to work and hated it. Or there simply wasn't enough money to go around. Or you're the first in your family to go to college or grad school – or earn six figures. It's a thrill, making it up there, conquering a new plateau of stability and social achievement. You want to bring everyone else up with you.

Or maybe this is what everyone's always expected of you because it's what they expected of themselves. You'll be like dad, or your father-in-law. They were The Providers in their day. They pulled it off. Why can't you?

It's easy to get sucked in. You'll have a big house, a few kids – maybe some leftover cash to lavish on mom and dad. "Let me fill your tank," you'll offer, without a care. "You deserve it."

The Provider wants to "have it all," "live the dream." That stuff.

If you try to be The Provider, you could wind up standing next to my client on the train platform at 7 am in a fat cat town like Greenwich or Stamford or Bronxville, clutching a briefcase, waiting for the express to Grand Central and your mid-town office.

That's okay. You want that, too.

It's later on, when things turn sour.

The partner drops a nightmare assignment on you, then takes off at 5 pm. Now you can't go home. By 11 pm, you're red-eyed and shaky in a mostly-empty office, fighting off a freak-out and trying to give that sonofabitch whatever it is he wants "on my desk tomorrow morning first thing." The hours tick by. You ache for home, for bed – like a normal person. At that point, The Provider doesn't care about the chunk of a purchase agreement that needs to be re-drafted, or that question about the indemnity clause that needs to be worked through. The Provider wants to collapse on the floor and sob.

When you call home to the wife to say you're stuck at work, she sounds patient, but annoyed.

At some point, your dreams bifurcated. She still wants all the stuff you used to want together. But now she wants more of it. Another child. A bigger house. Private schools. A vacation with the family to the Bahamas. A Mercedes. Summer camp for the kids.

You want to sleep – and to quit this god-awful job. But you know you can't. Ever.

This job, this miserable, thankless law firm job, makes her dream possible. This job makes The Provider possible. This job makes everything possible for everyone. Except you.

When you get home, you find himself yelling at the wife. She's pregnant with another kid – the second or third – and you're screaming at her that another kid was her idea and she doesn't understand you can't do it anymore and there isn't enough money and you don't want to go to your parents and ask for more money or let her parents pay for things because it makes you sick and why can't she stop and think before she promises to buy the kid an iPad for his 8th birthday, you can't afford it and why doesn't she get that through her thick skull!?!?

Then you slink off, pop a Xanax and attempt to breathe. The bad feelings come – remorse for being someone you don't want to be, the beast husband-father who screams and storms around the house and your little daughter looks scared of you, which hurts more than anything.

You fight the urge to pack a bag, get in the car, and drive.

You don't respect the wife. Maybe that's unfair. She keeps a clean house. She does the shopping. But there's a housekeeper. You pay for the housekeeper. And the wife sits at home with the kids and does her little part-time job, but that's it. When the weekend comes, she's complaining she has the kids all week, so it's your turn to take over. She needs to go out with her friends or she'll *lose her mind*. Then, in the middle of the night, the baby's squalling – and it's the same fucking thing – *she* takes care of the baby all day and *she* needs a break, so *you* should get up and try to make it stop screaming. Like *you* don't need a break? Like you get *any* fucking sleep? But that's unfair. You need to cool down. You don't know anymore. Is anything fair?

You have to stop yelling. That's not you. Keep your cool.

Kids need and need – that's what kids do, especially the baby. They can't care for themselves. But *she* has to do a something more, doesn't she? You're at that damned, god-awful, fucking miserable lousy law firm all day and night and she doesn't even know what that means. Why can't she get it through her head you can't take this anymore!

No one gets it.

How could anyone, who hasn't been there, imagine the misery of Biglaw? They think you're being dramatic; it's just a corporate job, right? The other husbands keep their cool. Why can't you snap out of it and do what's expected of you – what even *you* expected of you...

You tried lateraling into another firm. This job *is* the other firm. No one's making partner. The new plan is to go in-house eventually, but they want 10th years (because they can) and you're only a 7th year, and they want specialists (because they can) and you've changed "specialities" twice and at this point you know you're kidding yourself: You want out of law. But you have no idea what you really want to do. You were a fucking *Philosophy* major, for Chrissake. Nothing else would earn this money, which pays for... everything.

You look into the wife's eyes this morning and realize she thinks this is how it's supposed to be. Her father took the train into the City every day and earned a good salary so they lived nicely – like everyone else in town. He never made it such an ordeal.

She's keeping her end of the bargain. She puts up with you coming back after midnight and going in on weekends, stomping and snapping when you get home, refusing to do a simple thing like drive the kids to practice or get up when the baby cries – act like a father to your own kids.

The alliance is frayed. She's living a dream that's crumbled in your hands and run out between your fingers. You're anxious. All the time. That's the effect of a law firm.

You're also angry, very, very angry. It's supposed to be gratifying, being The Provider. But it's like slogging through a swamp, covered in leaches. Every single god-damned cent gone before you earn it. Enough with the accusatory looks. No, I'm not accepting money from your god-damned parents.

The Provider fantasy doesn't work – not for the lawyers I've met. Maybe an i-banker with fuck-you money can pull it off, or a rich doctor. A zillionaire partner. But they're on their second wife by the time they're forty. For most big firm lawyers, The Provider is a dead end. You stop wanting to do it, so you resent it. You want out of this box. Now.

You want to pack a bag, get in the car, and drive.

Re-frame your life as a series of conscious choices. Ask yourself if you want to be doing what you're doing.

But... But....

I know. You might have to scale things down. Your spouse might not like that. The kids might not like that.

You're not a golden goose. You're a person, not The Provider. If they don't see that reality, and recognize the price you're paying to protect them from the real world, then the Provider might actually pack a bag, hop in the car - and keep driving.

* * *

This piece was originally published on April 20, 2011 and triggered a flurry of comments. I was surprised that most of them came from women, who found themselves in the same trap I describe here - the role of The Provider. While I never intended to suggest The Provider was a gender-specific phenomenon, I had no idea this post would resonate so strongly with women attorneys. Apparently, having the husband stay home with the kids doesn't solve every problem – and it can create a few, as well.

Oh...that.

Associates at big law firms don't normally burn out right away. They arrive bright-eyed and bushy-tailed, raring to go. This is their moment! Grasp the golden ring!

If you look closely, though, you'll notice a few poor souls who burn out immediately – sometimes within a few weeks. These folks look awful almost from Day One, dread coming to work, don't talk to the others, can't sleep and wonder how to get out – like, immediately.

That's because they've been sexually harassed.

Oh...*that.*

Right. *That.*

I know. Sexual harassment is a drag of a topic, the stuff of tedious lectures by gender theorists and "Human Resource professionals." Nothing new to say, just standard material: wince-inducing scenarios, tired platitudes about respect and crossing the line and what's appropriate in a workplace blah blah blah...boring, scary, boring.

I hear about sexual harassment all the time from my clients, so it's a little less boring for me, and a lot more real. There is stuff worth talking about. But I'll keep it quick.

First, to be clear, I'm not talking about law firm sex in general. I'm as sex-positive as the next guy, and this isn't about sex. And I'm not naïve. I've heard all about the "hanky-panky" - ill-advised and otherwise - that goes on at firms. Associates get it on in their offices. Partners seduce young summers. Some of those partners are married. So are some of the summers. And it's not just a straight thing - gay associates and partners get caught up in this stuff, too.

When you're working together around the clock at a big law firm, there's a lot of pent-up sexual energy, so there's oodles of sleaze. Stuff happens. That stuff might be fun, or un-fun, no big deal or something you'll regret for a while. That's not our topic.

Harassment is never fun or okay. It's unwanted, unasked-for, undesired, unexciting, unpleasant, unsexy, unattractive, uncool sexual attention.

I have a theory that everything is more interesting if you stick the word "extreme" in front of it. Barbecue is okay. Extreme barbecue is way better. The same thing goes with sex. It intensifies things. Cool becomes super-cool if you add sex. Likewise, bummer turns into super-bummer if it's sexual. Harassment is a bummer, and sexual harassment is a super-bummer.

Here's what sexual harassment looks like:

- That overweight, bearded guy you could not be less attracted to – the young-ish partner with the photo of his wife and kids on his desk – leans over during a meeting alone with you in his office one evening and says "I'd really love to kiss you right now." And you're staring at a draft of a motion to dismiss and thinking you'd prefer to be anywhere else on Earth. And then he won't leave you alone. You start getting emails telling you how hot you are.

- The fratty, a-little-too-intense senior associate you found out you'll be reporting to next week gets drunk at the firm's new associates retreat and won't leave you alone. After the dinner, he invites himself along with you and some junior associate friends, then proceeds to act as though he's on a date with you, making double entendres and generally implying you have some sort of sexual relationship. It's embarrassing - and now you have to go into the office and face this freak who's supposed to be your new boss on a big case.

Welcome to sexual harassment. Yeah, it sucks. I wish it didn't. And there's no winning, either – no quick solution to make it go away. It's just a bummer all around.

Some of my clients try to ignore incidents, and get on with their lives. That might sound like a good idea, at least initially. The hope is everyone will pretend it never happened and move on. The problem is that guys who sexually harass the women they work with often don't stop after making jackasses of themselves once – they keep on making jackasses of themselves. The inappropriate stuff in his office or at the firm event turns into inappropriate stuff on the phone, on the trip to the deposition, or wherever and whenever.

Ignoring harassment also means you're ignoring the official procedure regarding harassment as promulgated by HR, which is to report it immediately. And it means everyone will ask you later why you didn't report it, and hold it against you and read into it and so on.

So eventually you will probably report it.

Now, in case I haven't made this clear, I'm a shrill, strident feminist. I totally, fully, utterly, 100% urge each and every woman who has been sexually harassed to feel fully empowered to report it. Every woman – every person - who shows the courage to take this step is a hero.

...but I can't pretend it doesn't suck. That's because everything about harassment sucks, including reporting it.

It is unpleasant and embarrassing, telling seriously up-tight law-firm senior partner types, whom you work for - the folks responsible for your bonuses and advancement - that some idiot (one of *them*, in fact) couldn't control himself and tried to kiss you during a meeting in his office.

And yes, the story will probably get around the firm, and probably embarrass and humiliate and perhaps piss off the guy who's been harassing you, and get him in trouble or even cost him his employment – which he richly deserves, especially if, as some of these guys do, he sort of threatened your job at some point with an idiot insinuation about how he'd hate to see you trying to transfer to another department because it could affect your chances of success at the firm (yes, that happened to one of my clients, and it was as shocking and hateful as it sounds.)

But it's no fun being the person who brings someone down when that someone works at your office, even if he was utterly inappropriate and deserves it. And it is no fun being at the firm when there are big, hush-

hush meetings and everyone is whispering and you are suddenly removed from all the cases you were working on with such and such senior associate or partner, and then you are suddenly moved to an office on the other side of the building or on a different floor, or he is, and everyone notices *that* and it's all they're talking about. And then you walk in the next morning and there he is – Mr. Harasser - standing in the elevator next to you but pretending he doesn't see you since he's under strict orders to leave you alone and you try to ignore him too and the whole thing is really weird.

And maybe now you can't do any anti-trust, or real estate work – which is why you came to that particular firm - because *he* was the head of that department, or he was the partner with all the work in that department. And maybe the firm is slow, so you go from having lots of work and plenty of billables to no work and no billables, which affects your bonus, or simply your chances to learn anything. And you can only wonder what your reviews are going to be like, now that you aren't doing anything and were pulled off everything you were doing right in the middle of it – and the guy who should be reviewing you was talking to you last week in his office alone about how he wants to see you in your underpants while you were trying to sort out an outline for a deposition.

And your friends keep saying you should have taped him, or written it all down and kept a precise paper trail and sued the firm and tried to get one of those settlements worth a few hundred grand, which would have paid off your debt and left you sitting pretty, even if it killed your legal career, which you think it might have done, or maybe not, who knows? In any case you didn't, and maybe you should have, but it still seems ridiculous to get rich because this idiot made a fool of himself. Maybe not. Who knows? People do it.

So you reported him, and it sucks... now what?

You wonder who you can talk to about it. There's your one pretty good friend at the firm, another female associate in your department - but she's the one who started all this by talking to HR after saying she couldn't stand listening to your stories of harassment. And you know she was right, and maybe you're relieved that she got it over with, but now she's looking at you like she wants to talk but you feel a wall has gone up, and somehow you don't want to talk about it with her anymore - you just want to *work* here, for a change, not be "harassment girl."

And there's the female partner, your "mentor" who logically should be someone you can talk to, but she's kind of, well, a bitch, and you feel – have always felt - she resents your existence at some level because you are young and pretty and oh, who knows – you just don't like her.

And there's the gay guy, the associate you met and have lunch with sometimes, who seems nice, but on the other hand, he doesn't really seem to care – he's got his own life.

And there's the HR lady who keeps saying you can always talk to her, but she looks like she's scared you're going to sue, like she's walking on eggshells.

And there's that nice older partner, but he's the one who decided it was appropriate to warn you not to let a senior associate into your room again, which seemed like blaming the victim - like you somehow should have known better and expected that creep would start getting weird. Maybe you *should* have known better. But shouldn't the creep have known better, too – isn't that the whole point?

And shouldn't any of the partners, maybe just once, have followed up and asked you how you're doing – which they never did, not once, as though everything were resolved, filed away and done – like there's an implicit suggestion you should feel that way, too, and if you don't there's something wrong with *you*?

And you don't think you can talk to your mom anymore – it only freaks her out and gets her all upset. And you don't even want to go there with dad.

So you talk to your therapist. And maybe he gets it. And working with him, you can start to get your head wrapped around this entire awful experience.

And now all you can think about is leaving. You've been at the firm a whopping two and a half months. Other people might hate it there too – but at least they had time to learn to hate it.

You want to go somewhere else, and start over, like none of this garbage ever happened. But the headhunter says you have to stay at least a year – and then good luck finding work as a second year.

Oh...*that.*

Yeah. It totally, totally sucks.

Originally published May 18, 2011.

Gone Fishin'

What is it about lawyers and vacations? Like the old saying about longhorn cattle and a Texas fence – they just don't get along so good. It's like a physical aversion.

I worked with a client recently who was planning, in utter frustration, to quit his medium-size firm in a medium-size American city. The partner was lecturing him about his billable hours, but business was dead slow so there was nothing to bill for. The lawyer found out later all his peers were billing for work that hadn't been done yet, on the theory they'd be laid off by the time the proverbial cow-patty and the fan were joined in unison.

He couldn't bring himself to fake his time records to that degree, so he was stomping mad, announcing to me in stentorian tones that this was it, he was quitting. I urged him to stick around and see if he couldn't get laid off with everyone else, so he could at least receive unemployment. No, he insisted – he needed out now.

Well, I reasoned, then why not take some vacation, so you can cool off and kill time simultaneously? That was unthinkable.

It turned out he hadn't had a vacation in 8 months – and *that* vacation was for 3 days.

Yes. THREE DAYS. Actually five, he said, since he took the weekend, too. He *took* the weekend.

His objection to taking a vacation now? He wasn't going out like that, on a sour note. That wouldn't be right.

125

So. Quitting in a huff was okay. But taking any of his accumulated vacation time when the firm was so slow there was nothing for anyone to do and everyone was faking their hours?

Inconceivable.

Flash forward six weeks. He didn't quit. Instead he managed to convince a partner to dump a bunch of work on him, and actually managed to approach the insane billable hours requirement for last month. Now he's totally exhausted, and his fellow junior associates are complaining he's hogging the work.

How about a vacation? I suggested.

No way. He'd just made his hours – how could he take a vacation now?

But isn't that the whole idea? That you've earned some time off?

He looked at me like I'd gone mad. If he took vacation now, all the other associates would get his work and he wouldn't be able to make his hours. Besides, if he took vacation, he'd have to work twice as hard.

Why? I asked. If you're off for two weeks of the month, you're only expected to work half as many hours, right?

Wrong. It doesn't work that way. You still have to make your hours for that month, even if you take a vacation. You just have to pull double-shifts.

Doesn't that defeat the whole point of taking a vacation?

He shrugged me off, exasperated. I didn't get it.

In the twisted mind of a lawyer, taking a vacation is simply bad. To take a vacation when the firm is slow rubs the unthinkable in their face – that the firm is slow. When things are busy? Well, then you're not pulling your weight, are you?

Of course, you can't simply "take" a vacation at a law firm – you have to clear it with the partner. At my client's firm, the standard response was: "this isn't a good time."

There is no good time.

One memory from Sullivan & Cromwell that's still etched into my brain after all these years is from my first vacation. I took a week to fly to England for New Year's and visit my old friend, Liz.

I arrived in Oxford exhausted and frazzled and settled into a comfy chair by the gas fire. Liz went to the kitchen to make a pot of tea. I heard the phone ring.

A moment later Liz re-appeared, looking puzzled.

"There's a terribly rude American woman on the phone who says she needs to speak with you right away."

It was a senior associate from S&C. I'd been at Liz' place for approximately 5 minutes. The associate berated me for some screw-up in a side agreement I'd worked on. It wasn't clear that it was my fault, and there wasn't anything I could do about it in England at 9 pm on Sunday night. But she needed to vent, so she called.

That's all behind me now. I'm a psychotherapist, and I take vacations.

For those of you who have written in wondering what's become of The People's Therapist – the answer is I'm taking a break. In-house counseling will return in all its glory to AboveTheLaw.com in September.

Until then, I'm enjoying some long weekends, working on a book project, and seeing my usual weekly caseload. For the first two weeks of August I'll be on my annual pilgrimage to Northeast Vermont, the land of dirt roads and pristine forests, where I'll hunker down in a cabin that's been in a friend's family for decades. There's no internet, no cellphone reception, no running water – nothing but serenity and a wood stove and a clear, deep pond. The cabin has one working rotary phone, but you'll have to let it ring a good while – we'll be out canoeing, or curled up with our dachshund on a hammock strung between two birches. I plan to read a stack of books, listen to plenty of Duke Ellington and fill my mind with ideas.

See you in September. Meanwhile...take a vacation. Please. Even lawyers can learn to relax if they try hard enough. You soul requires billable hours, too.

Originally published July 21, 2010.

The Golden Trough

When I summered at Shearman & Sterling back in the late '90s, the partners had just voted on whether to install a gym in the building or create a formal dining room.

Needless to say, they went with the dining room.

It was strictly lawyers-only. At the center stood a buffet fit for a cruise ship, replete with heaping chafing dishes. On certain days, they even had a "prime rib station," manned by a guy wearing a toque.

This was the golden trough. We fed with complete abandon - at least on days when we weren't being whisked off to The Four Seasons by a partner pretending to remember our names.

The joke was that all summer associates at Shearman gained 15 pounds.

It wasn't a joke. We did.

Almost overnight a relatively in-shape pack of law students morphed into a fresh, pudgy litter of big firm attorneys.

It's no secret law firms ply you with food to address the fact that they're denying you everything else. You're giving up a social life and working around the clock – but there's a smorgasbord only steps away, and free cookies in the conference rooms! If it gets really late (which happens a lot), you can order anything you want - anything! - from the seventy-five take-out menus stuffed in your secretary's desk drawer.

One late night at S&C, we decided to push the envelope. We all ordered take-out "surf-and-turf" platters. It was absurd – bleary-eyed associates tearing into steak and lobster tails with plastic forks and knives, sitting around a table cluttered with closing documents.

That was, admittedly, taking things to extremes. But eating at law firms is always something of a parody of a true dining experience. It amounts to exacting revenge for the fact of your presence there when you'd rather be anywhere else.

In my day at least, the financial printers was the ultimate example of what we used to call "punitive billing." They knew you resented spending your night in that place proofing offering documents – and the client was paying the bill. So they outfitted their proofing rooms like suites on a yacht, with menus elegantly bound between leather covers.

If you nodded in the direction of a printer employee at 1 am when he asked if he could get you anything, you'd probably end up with a $300 plate of sushi from the best Japanese joint in TriBeCa.

I know – it happened to me.

I stuffed myself until I felt ridiculous, then simply gave up. I hope somebody ate it.

Lawyers eat their anger. They pig out at the client's expense – or the law firm's - because they hate the way they're treated.

Ironically - and I know this because in the business world I dealt with outside counsel - clients resent how much their lawyers charge, and punish them by demanding insane deadlines and making them work nights and weekends.

The wheel of bad karma just keeps turning.

Born of that bad karma, the golden trough is filled with nothing but lame substitutes for the finer things in life – all the stuff you aren't getting, like nights off to share with your family and friends.

If you stare into the golden trough long enough, you'll fall in – and get fat. Then you'll lose one of life's truly fine luxuries – having a healthy, fit body you can feel proud of.

That's when the trough turns toxic.

I gained so much weight during my law firm years, I hardly recognized myself – and I wasn't the only one. There were plenty of other pale, chubby lawyers with dandruff on their suits, who needed haircuts and generally didn't seem to care what they looked like.

Let's face it: your life is out of your control in most regards when you work at a big law firm. But they aren't the ones putting food in your mouth. You can wake up and address your anger consciously. Instead of stuffing yourself to take revenge on your oppressor, focus your anger on a more productive outlet.

Refuse the trough – and hit the gym.

In my final months at S&C, I stopped eating food just because it was there, weight-trained five days per week and lost 35 pounds.

Now, more than a decade later, I maintain the same regimen. If I feel weak, I remember that fat guy in the ill-fitting suit. Never again.

Don't let them make you crazy - or fat. Refuse to be fed into submission. Turn your anger loose on the Stairmaster. Picture the face of that smug partner as you pump out another rep.

They can keep you there all night, but they can't turn you into a butterball. You can take your health, and your appearance back.

Nothing feels better than walking down the hall of a law firm feeling pumped and looking good. That partner can tear into your memo – but he's a fat lump, and you're starting to develop some nice cuts on your delts.

By all means, see a therapist. But mind and body go together, and endorphins are an excellent anti-depressant. Hiring a therapist is only half the job. He'll handle keeping your head in shape. You also need a trainer, or an aerobics or yoga instructor or a sports coach - someone to work on the rest of your body.

Never say I *should* get healthy. Never say I *need* to get healthy. Never say I'll *definitely* get healthy. ("Definitely" means "it's never going to happen.")

Say I want to get healthy.

To look good is to feel good.

* * *

I felt very old after I sent this column to my editor at AboveTheLaw (it originally ran on May 5, 2010) and she wrote back, asking what a "financial printer" was. It turns out everything is handled by email nowadays, or hosted on a website. Apparently, the great days of late-night pig-outs at the financial printers are a thing of the past.

The days of free fine cuisine at the big law firms are past as well, or so I heard from a number of older lawyers, many of them partners at big firms. One former S&C attorney told me they no longer pour the good champagne or offer heaping trays of oysters and peeled shrimp at their cocktail parties (more on that later...)

After I ran this piece I also received a flurry of comments from young lawyers asking why I was using old take-out menus from my secretary's desk. Hadn't I heard of the internet?

Well, in my day, junior, there was no internet. Or at least you didn't use it to order take-out food. And after I left S&C, I got a real life and stopped living on take-out food, so I never noticed you could order it on the internet.

I recently ran into yet another instance of feeling like a relic from another era. I was working with a client who was a corporate first-year, offering her advice on how to organize a closing table. I told her to leave plenty of time for the various officers to fax their signatures back and forth so she'd have everything executed properly in time for the money wire the next day.

She stared at me. It turns out they have some sort of "electronic signature" nowadays that makes the whole laborious exchange of faxed signatures unnecessary. Some new-fangled internet thingamabob. Harrumph. What will they think of next?

Better Get an Expert

I've always been awestruck by tax lawyers. They are the dudes.

As a transactional attorney, you can't make a move without a tax guy. He's the one who hands you a chart with boxes and arrows, holding companies and off-shore limited partnerships buying and selling and re-selling and issuing and repurchasing and spinning off. Everything starts there.

Tax lawyers do stuff no one else would even attempt – the *really* complicated stuff. They swagger out the door at 5 pm.

"Don't start with me. *I'm in tax.*"

Way back when, I took an advanced tax course in law school – just to see if I could roll with the gangstas. I even took it the wrong semester, so instead of JD candidates, it was LLM's snickering at my desperation. I received my lowest grade ever. I also discovered tax law is like higher mathematics: there *is* no big picture. Tax at the advanced level is not intuitive or guided by simple, over-arching principles; it's a mess of staggering, intimidating complication. You have to let go and trust in minds greater than your own.

What I've come to realize lately, as a therapist working with tax lawyers, is that these seemingly unapproachable superstars are human. And being "the expert" can exact a toll.

One guy – a senior tax lawyer from a big city firm – walked into my office last week. He had the usual frustrations. In an ordinary economy he'd be making partner soon, but business was terrible, so even the partners at his firm were being laid off. He was expecting a pink slip.

There was a deeper issue, too: He didn't like being a tax lawyer.

I gave him a speech about my admiration for his kind.

He appreciated the fawning worship, but his expression remained grim. "What you describe is actually what I hate about it."

It turns out being "the expert" can be isolating – and scary. From where he's sitting, there's incredible pressure to know everything and solve every problem.

He clued me in to his experiences, and in the process brought me down to Earth. Tax lawyers aren't a race of super-beings from Planet Krypton - tax is incredibly complicated for them, too. The job is about helping rich people avoid the IRS, which translates into "gaming" each tax law to create loopholes that the government closes up in the next version the following year.

There isn't just a "tax code," either. There's an endless labyrinth of fine print: contradictory court decisions, administrative regulations, IRS guidances, state and local and international consequences for every move you make...it goes on and on and on, twisting and turning like something from the imagination of Borges or Kafka.

The mind reels. At least my mind reels. I always believed that – by some miracle – if you were a tax lawyer, your mind didn't reel.

My client was a senior tax guy at a top firm. His mind was beginning to reel.

"They want to hear you say it's possible – whatever deal they dream up. So you're under massive pressure to find a way to do it. And it's all riding on you. If you screw up... I try not to think about it."

I thought about it. The entire deal blows up – probably in the papers. Millions of dollars lost by your client, who might try to sue you. Criminal penalties. Malpractice. Disbarment. All that bad stuff.

It's like writing an opinion letter. No lawyer wants to write an opinion letter. Why? The same reason no one wants to step into the sights of a high-powered rifle.

"I can't do this anymore," this guy said. "I feel like I'm wracking my brain, dealing with incredible complexity, holding on by my fingertips – all to save billionaires from paying their due."

It isn't only tax lawyers who end up "the expert." We had a bunch of experts at Sullivan & Cromwell. I remember an environmental guy whose only job was to review deals for pollution issues. There was an ERISA guy, too, who only reviewed stuff for ERISA issues (whatever they are). And there was a strange tall guy with a mustache who always smiled and whistled to himself. He was the '40 Act guy. I once sat through a CLE presentation he gave, and remember thinking it wasn't that I didn't understand the details - I couldn't figure out what the '40 Act was.

Sometimes the role of expert seems like a hot potato – everyone wants to pass it off to someone else. I remember doing a deal with AIG – some complicated nightmare with a dozen side agreements and sub-corporations selling and repurchasing their own holding corps. At the umpteenth drafting session, some banker scribbled down a formula on a napkin – no kidding, it was a mathematical formula, and he said "stick this in there." They'd been arguing for days about some clause in the back of the contract and this is what he told us to stick in there. I looked at it. There was what I recognized as a numerator, and a denominator, and a bunch of letters.

The partner glanced at it and told the of counsel to stick it in there. She handed it to me, and told me to stick it in there. I stuck it in there, but I didn't know what it was.

Of course, I knew the general rule that you're not allowed to put math into a contract, you have to put it into plain English. So that's what I tried to do: "the Pre-determined Selling Price shall be determined by a formula in which the numerator shall be the amount of the Settlement Price and the denominator shall be one added to the amount of the Sales Price multiplied by the First Pre-Settlement Price minus the square root of the Third Sub-Corporation Preliminary Offering Variable..."

You get the idea. I had no idea what I was doing. I tried, a few times, inserting numbers, just to see what would happen. The first time I got something like one hundred billion dollars. I knew I'd done something wrong. The second time I got something like 0.000125782 dollars.

I should add that it was late at night and I'd been wearing the same wool suit for seventeen hours.

I gave up and handed it nonchalantly to the of-counsel. No biggie. I'd "taken a stab at it." She might yell at me, but she'd know what to do. If she had to, she'd fix it herself.

But she didn't.

I watched her disappear into the partner's office, then return. Her face was set. She approached my desk and plopped the offending passage down in front of me.

"Just double-check this and make sure it's right. Thanks."

I knew right away what had happened. The partner had no idea what the damn thing was either, so they passed it back to me. I'd bragged once about my brother, the nuclear physicist, so maybe they thought I could do math. And this little nightmare was in the last page of a side agreement. It was indecipherable. It wasn't that important. It would probably never matter. I wasn't about to create a fuss, so I pretended to "look it over" and left it in whatever shape it was when they gave it back to me.

I still have no idea what it was or how it worked, but it is buried somewhere deep in an agreement on the books of AIG Corporation. I think we can all agree that AIG is a stable, trusted cornerstone of the American economy, and there's zero chance of AIG ever experiencing financial distress. So relax. We're fine.

That's the essence of being "the expert." As a lawyer, you're "counsel." You're supposed to know everything. You're also supposed to be risk-averse and spot every possible problem before it happens, and be able to predict the future. And you're supposed to "know the law" - as though anyone could ever really "know the law." And you're supposed to make it happen – whatever it is – for your client. Some of those goals are impossible – or at least mutually exclusive. So you start to fake it. And that's what happened to that tax lawyer I was working with. He was feeling more and more like a fake, and he wanted to run away and hide.

I've seen it before. One of my clients was a partner at a medium-size firm in a medium-size city who told me about his "garbage can deals" - the ones where you throw it all into a contract and get the thing closed – slam a lid down on whatever's in there - then hope no one ever opens it back up. Every lawyer who's ever done a few deals knows he has a garbage can deal in there, but he'd probably never admit it. After all – he's the expert. He must know what he's doing.

At some level, it's a big fake-out. Posing as the guy who knows everything can make you rich. Or land you in jail. Or keep you up at night.

Originally published February 16, 2011.

Brain Dead

There's slow at the office. Then there's moribund. Like, stick a fork in it, parrot in the Monty Python skit, no longer viable, kaput, over and out, flat-lining...dead dead dead.

Like you haven't recorded a billable hour in weeks. Like you show up at 10:30 am, slide your Kindle under your computer monitor and try to look busy while you read John LeCarre novels. Then leave at 6 pm – or whenever the coast is clear and you think you can get away with it.

We all know having nothing to do at a big law firm is better than being busy. Being busy is really, really bad. When you're really busy, you know you will have to quit soon because you can't bear it, and when the loans get sufficiently below $100k that will be your cue to say fuck it, I need out.

But when you're totally dead at the office, you think...hmmm...might as well wait on the bailing out and keep those delightful loan-reducing paychecks coming in, right?

No one ever leaves because it's too slow. You wait it out. Pay off loans. And wait. And do nothing. And wonder if the partners are noticing – or whether they somehow don't realize you haven't billed an hour since 1971.

One of my clients was deep in a Kurt Vonnegut novel when a partner dropped by his office.

"Your billables are a little low this month," the partner opined.

My client threw on his "sincere face" - a complex intermingling of dignified concern at the immediate reality presented to him in the here and now and a more generalized melancholy at the state of the world as a whole, with emphasis on the wider suffering that exists everywhere – suffering he himself is helpless to address.

"Yes, it has been a bit quiet. I'm doing what I can to make myself helpful wherever I can, but..." He let his voice trail off, helpfully.

The partner frowned, apparently in deep thought.

"I'll let the Banking Group know. They'll be contacting you."

And so my client spent the rest of the week facing the looming dread that "the Banking Group" would contact him. Happily, they never did. He relaxed back into his familiar daydream-like stuporous trance state. Two weeks later, he's charting the intricacies of "Freedom" - the Jonathan Franzen novel, and contemplating a switch to an iPad to read "Infinite Jest," the 1000-page David Foster Wallace behemoth, since it's easier to tackle long footnotes on an iPad than a Kindle. This has been the topic of much discussion with his officemate, who also has nothing to do but has been progressing through multi-volume classics of the vintage sci-fi/fantasy genre. Somehow, he'd never gotten around to reading the complete Dune series or Frederik Pohl's HeeChee saga. That's since been rectified. Next up: Asimov's Foundation series.

Deadness at the office is good. You don't have to work, you just log face time. Also, there's a chance you'll get laid off, maybe with one of those heavenly "soft landings" where the firm gives you three months paid (while you do precisely nada) before they show you the door. That's three more months of paying down loans...

Busy time at a law firm obviously sucks – there's no debate there. But dead time has drawbacks as well.

Perhaps the ideal would be some weird mix of busy and dead – like, halfway busy. That would be like...a regular job. You know, coming in at 9 am, working on something, then leaving at 5 pm.

That doesn't exist in law. It could never exist.

No, there are two dichotomous possibilities – the hell of busy, and the better but still problematic dead. Dead is much better, even though it sucks. But then anything at a big law firm sucks, so better to have it be dead and have that suck than be working eighty hour weeks and have that suck infinitely more.

These are the kinds of thoughts you process when it's dead at the office.

Long, twisty, repetitive time-killing thoughts. You calculate the exact day on which you could, theoretically, achieve zero net worth. Then you wonder what would happen to that date if there were a bigger bonus this year. Or no bonus.

There is one major hazard to having it be completely dead at the office, which is that your brain may die. At some point a senior associate from another department who doesn't realize you haven't billed an hour in months will walk up to you and try to talk about "law" and you will look up from page 673 of "Infinite Jest" and hear his mouth emitting the following sounds:

"Mrrrphph schlurphph loan agreement murrrpslurphh snurphphffffpff credit mezzanine schrluphphfff...

You will gape at him and open and close your mouth like a fish lying on ice waiting to be someone's dinner and try to remember what it was like being a fish, swimming around in the ocean and looking for little bits of the stuff floating in the water that fish eat....What is that stuff? Plankton? Krill? Brine shrimp? Tiny squid larvae...?

But wait. He's still talking to you. What is it about? Does it concern work? Law? Vague, shadowy memories of distant concepts swim in your mind like a cloud of...uh...krill.

"Mrrrphph schlurphph loan agreement murrrpslurphh snurphphffffpff credit mezzanine schrluphphfff..."

It's... resolving slowly...into something. A question. A question of some variety. Who is this person again? Where are you? A law firm? How did you get in a law firm?

Your mouth is opening and closing. Something is coming out. The senior associate appears perturbed, or worried. Unhappy. That's it. He's unhappy.

"Mmmmmm....gggggoooooooo....schchchcllllooooooshnnooop," you are saying.

And he leaves. And you return to your computer, and the iPad tucked beneath it.

Not working for weeks at a time, or months at a time, will destroy your brain. You will forget anything you ever learned in law school. You will grope fecklessly at knowledge you thought you'd gained in elementary school. To outsiders, you will begin to appear "learning disabled."

There's another hazard. You will forget that work could ever be anything other than the thing you are glad you are not doing. That's what happens when it's totally dead at the office. You forget how to do work – in fact, you forget how to think.

Then you forget you want to do work.

The most destructive element of the big law trap is that it destroys the dignity of work. First, the labor of your body and mind is reduced to a billable hour. Then it is exploited until it becomes physically and mentally unbearable. Then it is taken away, and relief floods your system.

Then you find you are phobic to the notion of work. You loathe it. You seek only to avoid it.

All you want is for someone to pay the loans and leave you alone.

That's a tragedy, because work is more than something unpleasant you do to pay off loans – or try to avoid while still trying to pay off loans.

Work is an expression of who you are. It is what you create during your time on Earth. It lends meaning to your days. Please – don't confuse the law grind with a career, or with meaningful work. One phenomenon bears no relation to the other.

Law sucks, and it might be killing you to be in debt for decades to come. But there is a role out there, a place in human society that will fulfill something deep within you. It's the reason you're here, alive, in the world. There is a goal you want to reach – a dream you want to catch.

You'll get out of that damn firm. You'll pay off those loans, some day – or at least reduce them to a bill each month, like any other bill.

Don't let law destroy the meaning of work for you. Don't let it make you give up on the dream of doing something you love and making a difference.

Law might make you feel like your brain is dead. Don't let it break your heart as well.

Originally published June 1, 2011.

Both Sides Now

My client was a hard-boiled commercial litigator, a junior partner. "When you want a street fight, call me in," was one of her mottos. She won cases. She made a lot of money. She kicked ass.

She was having issues with a second year associate.

At first, they got along. The associate was bright, and wanted to impress. The problem was deeper. As the partner put it bluntly: "She just isn't cut out for this place."

Yeah. That old line. But now I was sitting with the partner who was saying it, nodding my head in agreement.

Here was the situation:

The associate grew up working class - a smart big fish in a small pond. She expected to compete and win, like she always had. Her aim at the firm was to show everyone she was the smartest one there. So she worked endless hours, volunteered advice before she was asked, and chatted about French films at lunch.

The partner hated her. It felt like a competition instead of a working relationship. She complained the associate "didn't understand her place in the pecking order" and failed to show respect by deferring to the partner's experience. A street fighter didn't waste time competing with a kid to write an erudite brief – she could mop the floor with her in a courtroom.

Things came to a head when the partner reviewed a document with obvious typos and sent an email to the associate, saying – hey, did anyone check this thing before it went out?

She got back a half dozen outraged paragraphs: The partner never appreciated the associate's work or the long hours she was putting in; she was arrogant and inconsiderate; she had no idea how to manage others; she didn't know as much law as she thought. It concluded with a threat: if the partner didn't want to work with her, she'd be happy to work with someone else.

The partner wasn't sure what to do. The email was inappropriate and if anyone else saw it, would go over (as they say in Mississippi) like a fart in church. This wasn't how things were done. Not at her firm.

She asked me what I thought.

The best plan seemed to be a gentle approach. Remind the associate she'd done good work, and that her abilities and dedication were appreciated, but make it clear the email was inappropriate. We talked over various approaches, and what needed to be said. The partner kept reminding me it didn't matter how many hours you worked, if you were sending stuff out to clients with obvious typos.

She had a point. The associate needed to understand that wasn't acceptable. The big message, in her mind, was make sure it doesn't happen again.

Something else itched at her, too - the associate needed to stop taking this kind of thing personally – to buck up, and get on with the job.

Even as we talked over the partner's response, I realized there was a bigger problem: these two people don't like one another, and that associate doesn't belong at that firm.

I know my client – we've worked together for months. I understand her side of things. But I see a lot of myself in the associate, too, and her predicament feels all too familiar.

Sometimes I feel like I'm standing in the middle, seeing both sides.

The partner is a pro. She grew up with a father who was himself a wealthy Big Law managing partner, and she thrives on the slightly frat boy-ish, hazing aspect of the commercial litigation world. She suffered through being a junior associate herself, but caught another partner's eye early on, and earned her stripes. In her view, if you don't like going for the jugular – a good dirty brawl – then you don't belong there. The firm is a club, and she's in that club, and she likes it that way.

Is she perfectly happy in her career? No. The grueling hours mean her personal life is, as she puts it, "a work in progress." That mostly translates into abortive flings with other attorneys (some at her firm) and drunken hook-ups she typically regrets. She isn't thrilled about being single, has mostly given up on kids and isn't even sure she wants a family. But she loves her work, and if she has to spend too much time at a job, this is where she wants to do it. She has her Upper West Side two-bedroom, and her cat, and she takes nice vacations – active stuff, like skiing or horseback riding with tour groups of other wealthy, single women. She dotes on her nieces.

I never met the associate, but I could fill in the blanks from what the partner told me. She lives with her unemployed PhD boyfriend in a tiny apartment in Brooklyn, and is carrying both their school loans. He seems resentful that she's never around, and they hardly ever have sex anymore. She hates the firm, but has no choice since jobs are hard to come by and they both have loans. She tells herself she has to succeed at this job, and she does everything they ask, including putting in brutal hours - but nothing seems to work. She does a lot that's right, and never hears a kind word – but if she makes a stupid mistake from sheer exhaustion, she never hears the end of it. Lately, after arriving home at 11 pm feeling like a zombie, she wonders if she can force herself to return the next morning for another round of abuse.

She doesn't like them, and they don't seem to like her. When she tries to raise the tone once in a while, and talk about film or literature - anything beyond civil procedure and televised sports - it falls flat. The partners are a bunch of frat boys – even the women - caught up in winning pointless commercial litigation cases so they can get drunk on bottle service in TriBeCa and wind up in bed with each other. The cases are all about making money for millionaires, and she isn't seeing any of it, so why should she care?

One interesting aspect of my job is that I hear both sides of the story.
I have several clients like that partner – and many in the same position as that associate. There is no right or wrong here – no good guy or bad guy. At the end of the day, the partner belongs in that job, and the associate doesn't.

When the partner asked a more senior partner at the firm for advice about how to handle the associate, he cut to the chase: "it doesn't matter what you tell her – she won't last long anyway."

That's probably true – at least the second part. But the partner wanted to do the right thing. One half of her ached to tell this kid to wise up, to snap out of it and "grow a pair." It was the kind of thing she was used to hearing – all in fun, and the spirit of the firm. But something told her it wouldn't work. To this associate, it would only sound cruel. She eventually toned it down instead, trying to sound supportive, but even she could hear the impatience in her voice - and see the anger etched on the associate's face.

They came from different worlds. Maybe it didn't matter what the partner said to the associate. It wouldn't make much difference.

She wasn't going to last long, anyway.

* * *

I felt like I was taking a big risk with this piece, which was originally published on December 1, 2010. Instead of pushing any particular agenda, I hoped to express how it feels to be in my shoes as a therapist working with lawyers from both sides of the associate/partner divide, standing in the middle, trying to see – and understand – where both are coming from. As things turned out, I also, inadvertently, tackled some of the sexual politics of the law firm world. Many of the responses I received to this piece addressed the friction between women who are trying to keep relationships going despite the stresses of law firm life – and those who have sacrificed lasting relationships for success at their jobs.

Work/Life Whatever and Ten Missing Minutes of Tape

I did a podcast a while back with the American Bar Association Journal. The topic was "work/life balance." You can listen to it on their website.

It was a weird experience – like living on another planet.

I was the sole male. The other panelists and the moderator were women. That's fine, but somehow, faced with the topic of "work/life balance" everyone turned into Gloria Steinem circa 1971.

Don't get me wrong. I'm a shrill, strident feminist committed to full equality for women, and I have no beef with Gloria Steinem.

But how is work/life balance in the legal world strictly a gender issue? Women are admitted to law schools, and graduate from them, like men. They go to the same law firms, make the same money and take the same abuse.

I have tangential experience with this stuff since I'm gay. When people talk about homophobia at Sullivan & Cromwell I roll my eyes. Homophobia wasn't the issue. Humanophobia was the issue. Some of the partners and plenty of the associates were openly gay. Homo or hetero, male or female we were all in the same boat.

The unspoken "women's lib" angle on the "work/life balance" at law firms is this: women give birth to children, and it's impossible to raise a kid if you are a partner at a law firm, so women are less likely to become partners. If they did, they wouldn't have time to raise a kid. It's also impossible to meet anyone you want to have a kid with when you're working 70-hour weeks.

These are incontrovertible facts of law firm life.

Plenty of male partners have kids. They become absentee fathers, and their kids never see them. Nothing new there. But a social stigma kicks in when your kid tells his friends he only sees mommy an hour a week.

You also have to find time to be pregnant. If you put it off until you make partner, you face fertility problems. That's a fundamental bummer about being a woman who wants a kid - when you're mentally prepared your body gives out. At sixteen, anyone can get pregnant. At thirty-nine, you can only get pregnant if you don't want to. If you're trying, it never happens.

The solution to all this is obvious – have a kid while you still can, and let your husband do the raising.

That's more or less where the other panelists ended up, but only after spouting "women can have it all" slogans and fabricating visions of "part-time partners." The law professors on the panel had no concept of law firm reality. The young lawyer running an internet-based T&E firm receded politely when I pointed out the obvious: plenty of women would rather stay at home with the kids than work at a firm. Heck, I've worked with couples where the husband and wife fight over who has to do law for a living. They'd *both* rather stay home and play with junior. Wouldn't you?

A second yawning gulf between me and the other panelists came with their determination to defend law as a profession. They were "pro-law" and I was "anti-law." That's understandable, since the ABA Journal represents the official propaganda ministry for Law, Inc. Law professors need to herd eager young things into school – that's how they earn big bucks. And the internet lady was trying to drum up business, too - she has loans to pay.

I'm not from that world. I'm a psychotherapist who cleans up the wreckage of young lives decimated by the law school/law firm machine.

Here's a little scandal for you: at least ten minutes of the podcast – the final ten minutes, where I stopped sitting back feeling out of place and came out swinging - were deleted from the recording. You hear a fadeout as I'm about to come on.

What did you miss?

You guessed it – a whole lot of me talking about the reality of law firm life – and lawyer unemployment – including the fact that "work/life balance" is a myth for most lawyers because they work insane hours and hate their jobs.

In other words, a cool, clear blast of truth.

Why is work/life balance a myth? For starters, the billable hour.

A headhunter called one of my clients last week. Familiar with the routine, she picked up for the heck of it, wondering how they'd manage to spin an obscure mid-level firm into a paradise where no one worked past 6 pm and the walls were made of chocolate. The sales reptile on the phone didn't disappoint.

"You'll love this place – it's a lifestyle firm. They only expect 2200 hours per year!"

My client had to smile at how far things have come. 2200 hours per year, with two weeks of vacation, equals forty-four hours per week of billables. Which means you're probably working a fifty hour week.

So that's a "lifestyle" firm – you're only there ten hours per day. And that's if you believe a headhunter. In real life you'd almost certainly be there weekends as well.

My client told me another story, about a friend who woke up and realized she had to quit law – she was failing as a spouse, failing as a mother and failing as an attorney. She called it the "three failures theory."

Then my client got up early herself one recent morning to crawl back into the office after a late-nighter. On her way out the door she stepped – wearing new pumps – in a massive puddle of cat pee. That's because, working 2200 hours or more per year, she hadn't changed the kitty litter. That was her one household undertaking – her husband, who worked a normal job, did all the other chores. She screamed in frustration. Her husband came rushing to her rescue, asking why she hadn't changed the litter. She lost her temper, yelled "I don't have time for this crap!" and, of course, was late for a meeting at her firm.

The theory of three had been fulfilled: failing as a spouse, failing as a kitty mommy, and failing as a lawyer.

It was time to get out.

Here's my bottom line. Work/life balance is impossible so long as the billable hour remains the holy grail of firm life. Working "only 2200 hours per year" makes it impossible to have a family or any sort of personal life.

Sorry. That's the truth.

And that's what I was saying in those missing ten minutes of tape that got cut.

In years to come, you'll probably be treated to a few hundred fresh hours of Richard Nixon's tape-recorded disquisitions on the racial inferiority of blacks and Jews – but if the ABA Journal has its way, you're never going to hear those last ten minutes of why it sucks to be a lawyer.

* * *

This piece was originally published January 12, 2011. No, I never complained to the ABA Journal about their cutting those ten minutes from the podcast. But it riled me - I was shocked when the voices suddenly faded as I was about to address important issues. Maybe I'm not ready for prime time – or the legal profession isn't prepared to face a real crisis affecting real lawyers leading real lives.

Working for The Man

In law, if you're making big money, you're working for the bad guys. That's the sad truth.

I'm not talking about defending vicious criminals. I mean tougher cases - like representing the one percent of the world who own everything.

Deep in the recesses of big law, you might not realize who you're really working for. From where you're standing, your boss is the firm. Juniors report to seniors. Seniors report to partners. Partners report to God.

In reality, up, over the partner's head, there's someone called "the client" - a possessor of vast wealth. Normal people don't hire Biglaw – the owners-of-everything do, and they don't get über-rich being nice. Things only get worse when they're dealing with their lawyers.

If and when you actually meet "the client," you might feel like an Imperial Stormtrooper aboard the Death Star:

Lord Vader? Great to meet you, Sir. Yes, absolutely, the torture chamber is looking shipshape. Yes sir, we just checked the planetary death ray this morning. One hundred percent ready to go. My pleasure, Sir.

Then the client walks away, and you play that same argument in your head: You have one hundred and seventy grand in school loans. They're going to blow the planet up anyway. You're not torturing anyone *personally*.

Some lawyers learn to embrace the evil – to "go with it." I knew a guy in law school who left to work for a firm that did nothing – NOTHING – but defend Big Tobacco. We ribbed him about it. In fact, we regarded him as a stinking pile of vomit. His response was to chain-smoke and brag about the money. He disappeared to work black voodoo in a hateful red state - by now he's probably worth millions. Loathed by millions, too.

My first taste of evil came early at Sullivan & Cromwell. It was a deal for Goldman Sachs with an amusing codename: "Project Rolex." At the closing I finally encountered the client - and the wry humor of i-bankers: He wore the largest gold wristwatch ever made.

I developed a fascination with Mr. Rolex. His name was all over documents I'd been staring at for weeks. The deal – a securitization of mortgages on a package of investment properties in the Southwest – suburban strip malls and industrial parks – was worth half a billion dollars. As I generated documents, I took guesses at his net worth. If it wasn't a billion, it was darn close. A journalist who met Bill Gates at a technology convention once wrote a piece admitting all he could think about while they shook hands was "$500 per second. $500 per second. $500 per second." Same thing with this client: I couldn't believe how much money he made.

After weeks of late nights, the partner asked me to arrange catering for the closing. The choice was the standard Sullivan & Cromwell breakfast with rolls and bagels or the "deluxe" breakfast, with lox. For Mr. Rolex, I pulled out the stops and ordered deluxe.

He stormed into the room the next morning, sporting a cowboy hat, cowboy boots and the giant gleaming timepiece. I was awestruck.

But Mr. Rolex was not in a good mood. He turned to the partner: "This is no good. I can't sign all this shit. I'll be here all day, you fucking asshole."

Apologies were mumbled. It *was* a lot of paperwork. On the other hand, the client was mortgaging about 400 commercial properties, most worth millions. We'd been generating paperwork day and night for weeks.

Rolex eventually relented, mumbling obscenities, and started signing. He whipped out the largest gold pen ever made and circled the tables, shouting into a cell phone.

Here's what a man worth half a billion dollars shouts while he signs documents earning himself another half a billion dollars:

"Brenda. Tell that fucking pilot at Teterboro to hold the fucking plane. Don't be a fucking idiot, just do it. Tell him I don't fucking care. And put the right fucking food on it. I can't eat that shit. Assholes. I'll tell you what

150

to do about Jeff. Put his fucking shit out on the lawn and take his fucking keys. Dan, too. Lock them out of the fucking building. Fuck their families. They're fucking fired. I don't know when I'll be fucking back. What are you, retarded? These fuckers are wasting my fucking life. This is bullshit. No – he's fired, too. I don't give a crap...."

It took our client less than an hour to "execute" the documents. He shouted "fuck" three dozen times, fired five people, then stormed out of the room.

We stood in silence. I began helping the paralegals gather up the papers. We ate the deluxe breakfast.

The next day, the partner told me never to order the deluxe breakfast again without prior clearance. The client refused to pay the extra hundred and fifty bucks.

There can be no doubt Mr. Rolex left his mother's womb screaming abuse into a cell phone. There is no possibility he was ever a nice person. He made me feel sorry for the partner – who, himself, was not a nice person.

Your client might not be floridly evil like Mr. Rolex. He might be boringly, namelessly evil. Most litigators tell me their clients are anonymous banks suing or being sued over anonymous ill-fated investments. They know perfectly well these banks are run by mountebanks who merrily screw their clients because they only care about making money for themselves. If these litigators drilled deeper, to find out who owned the anonymous banks, they'd find Mr. Rolex sputtering into a cell phone – but they don't want to go there.

One of the joys of earning less money at law is working for the good guys, or the less-bad guys. You get to help people who actually need it.

I worked with a Biglaw lawyer who recently left for the SEC, thrilled to be protecting investors instead of i-banks. On the other hand, I worked with a guy who left the FTC for Biglaw, and found himself defending the same sleazy supplement manufacturers he used to prosecute. Needless to say, the first lawyer was happier - but working for evil pays better.

It's a trade-off. Everything's a trade-off. But it's worth something to know you're on the side of the good guys. Maybe that's a luxury, if you've got loans to pay. But it's also a goal to shoot for while keeping your eyes on the ultimate prize: doing work that means something to you.

* * *

I took a beating in the comments for this column, which was originally published on March 16, 2011. Readers accused me of generalizing unfairly about the wealthy – i.e., claiming they're all evil - which smacked of socialism to some. Those readers may have been taking this piece a bit too seriously – it was intended to be humorous. On the other hand, they had a point - working with zillionaires as a Biglaw lawyer didn't leave me a fan of the super-rich. I met quite a few unsavory clients during my time at S&C who made me wish I were working for the deserving poor instead of following my wallet wherever it led.

Where You Eat

Office romances are endemic in the legal profession - I encounter them constantly with my clients. Why is there so much fooling around at law firms? Triangulation. A partner in a couple "triangulates" - looking to a third party to replace what's missing in his relationship. For lawyers, "what's missing" boils down to time spent together.

One married lawyer told me she flirts with a junior associate at her office. She loves her husband, but never sees him. Flirting with the junior satisfies her craving for sexual attention. Lately, though, they've been going out for drinks, and she's afraid something will happen she'll regret.

Single lawyers experience the same romantic isolation. One said she hadn't been to a bar or club – let alone a party – for over a year. She keeps canceling dates because of work, and her friends no longer ask her out because she always declines. This month she's been working late nights with another associate at her firm and they've started hooking up.

Most human beings divide their days in three equal parts: You work. You play. And you sleep.

Lawyers sleep – sometimes. But they don't play – they just work. Then they work some more.

When work replaces play, you find yourself playing at work: taking Facebook breaks, browsing blogs... or letting things turn jiggy with co-workers.

Is there a problem with getting it on at the office?

If you're married, or in a committed relationship, the answer is easy: yes. That's because, if you're sleeping around, you're lying to someone. There's nothing sacred or holy about monogamy - but you can't have your cake and eat it too. You wouldn't want someone to lie to you, so you shouldn't lie either.

For single lawyers the issues are subtler, but the answer is still yes, there is a problem, because combining your romantic life with your workplace life creates unavoidable conflicts.

The dysfunction created by a law firm romance is epitomized by the archetypal hook-up between a 40-something male partner and a 20-something female associate. I see it all the time, and yes, sometimes it's a female partner and sometimes it's between two men or two women. Doesn't matter - it's still a train wreck.

The partner is riding out a power trip. He's on his second or third wife, using status and money to avoid other issues like personal insecurity and fear of commitment.

The associate gets a rush of power, too. Suddenly she's the center of attention for a guy earning seven figures – and he's hinting things are falling apart with the wife.

Two big problems...

First, exploitation. I don't care if he's sexy and powerful and paying you a lot of flattering attention and doesn't seem like such a bad guy. There's a massive power differential and that equals exploitation. Controlling an associate's every waking hour and earning twenty times her salary ought to suffice to satisfy this guy's need for attention. Sleeping with that associate crosses a line that shouldn't be crossed.

Second, role confusion. Roles exist to keep boundaries clear. The associate is an employee. The partner is first and foremost her boss. He decides what work she does, how much she does of it and how much she's paid. He might decide whether she can take a vacation. Theoretically, he teaches her how to be a better lawyer. At the end of the day, he decrees whether she's any good. It confuses everything if he's also feeling up her breasts in the back seat of the black car.

Eventually, in these situations, things come to a head, and work and play collide. Like when he dumps her because he and his wife are "giving it another chance" and she freaks out and refuses to come into work for a few days. Or when she calls it off with the partner because she's met someone her own age, and a few weeks later, the partner gives her a bad review and jeopardizes her job. I've seen these scenarios play out too many times.

Partners should not be sleeping with associates at their firms. It's unprofessional and un-cool. If he wants to pursue a relationship, he can get to know you first, then help you transfer to another firm.

Run of the mill law firm romances, without the difference in age or power, rarely work either. There might not be the element of exploitation, but role confusion manages to muck everything up.

Sex creates an intimate connection, even if you're both doing your damnedest to ignore it. Someone feels a connection – maybe both of you do. If it doesn't work out – and most hook-ups don't turn into anything more – one of you is going to feel rejected. There could be strong unresolved feelings. That situation turns especially uncomfortable when that guy it didn't work out with is also the of-counsel who's handling a super-important deposition with you, or the junior helping you prepare a $400 million securities issuance.

Working together – putting in long hours in a competitive environment – can be a challenge, and romantic relationships are tough to pull off under the best of circumstances. Combining workplace and relationship issues is asking for trouble.

Some boundaries are worth respecting.

Originally published April 28, 2010.

Not Horrible

I asked a client how things were going at work – or not-going. She's a junior at a big firm where it's been dead slow for the whole year she's been there and partners are starting to flee.

"Not horrible," she said.

That's a not-uncommon sentiment, coming from someone in her position. As a junior, you're asking for not-much. You've realized law school was a mistake - and the thought of your loans makes you queasy. If you get through the day without being criticized or given some god-awful assignment, you can go home and try to sleep. That's a good day.

Not-horrible means not-unbearable, even if you hate what you're doing, see no way out and cry alone in your office.

Not-horrible is not-unemployed. Better to not-complain.

One junior associate client has a corporate headhunter friend, who asked him to write something down and commit it to memory:

"There. Are. No. Jobs."

Okay. Got it.

Another client spoke for thousands when he said he hates the thought of waking up and facing another day at his firm, but with two hundred grand in loans, how can he leave a job where he isn't working that hard and earns $160k?

"The partner's a psychopath – don't get me wrong. He expects me to answer the Blackberry at 2 am and criticizes every move I make. But he's paying me a fortune to take this crap, right?"

Hey, it's not horrible.

The week before Thanksgiving, my client reminded this partner he'd be away for the actual day of the holiday – Thanksgiving Day – to visit his wife's family.

The partner looked shocked at this effrontery.

"Will you be available remotely?" he asked.

"I'll be available anally, if that helps," were the words my client struggled not to utter. Because that would have gotten him fired.

"Of course," is what he actually said.

Hey, it's not horrible.

At a big law firm, it's hard to imagine a life containing meaning or pleasure. This is a legal career: You exchange human misery for money, which pays loans.

One client's firm has a "free market" policy, so each associate competes for work. That way, if you admit to another junior that you don't have any work, it invites him to look relieved and announce he does. My client isn't sure which is worse – not having work and having nothing to do or having work and having to do it. Mostly, she does nothing, and suspects the others do, too – but no one tells anyone anything.

It's not horrible.

I hear this one from lawyers all the time: "It's no better anywhere else, is it?"

But you know it is. Outside of law. The entire world isn't as bad as a law firm just because you're stuck in one. As they say in Alcoholics Anonymous – it's simple, but it's not easy. To escape not-horrible you just have to escape law. That's the not-easy part.

Not-horrible is a holding pattern - you might be stuck there for a while. That's what the loans are for. In the old days they used chains.

Does not-horrible ever end?

Yes. Here's why: they'll get rid of you.

If it's not-horrible, you're probably not-busy, because if you were busy, it would be horrible. You're also probably not into it. If you were into it, you'd be trying to make partner, which would be horrible, but you wouldn't be saying it's horrible. You probably wouldn't be saying it's not-horrible, either.

So, if you're not into it, and it's not busy, you're not going to last more than two years. The general rule is, if you're sitting around not-doing anything and not-billing an hour for about four months, you will not get laid off. If it's that slow, the firm is not-stable and they're not-worried about you – they're not-noticing your existence. Not-keeping you only draws attention to the larger problem of their not-flourishing as a going enterprise.

But if you're not-expecting to be fired, you will be. Suddenly. When you most not-expect it.

In any case, you're not going to last more than two or maybe three years, because at some point, if things are not-horrible, you're not-there. If you stay at a firm for two or three years and things are not-horrible and you are not-there, then you are not-learning, or learning mostly not-law. (This column is an example of not-law.) Not-learning means reaching third-year knowing as much as a first-year. You wind up a not-lawyer.

You "ran changes" in documents. You "did doc review." You wrote a memo. It was not-read.

You sat around, mostly, trying to not-communicate that you're freaking out. They'll get rid of you. It's a matter of time.

So the question becomes – what do you do then, when you wake from the long stupor of not-horrible and sit up, dazed, uncomprehending - a not-employed not-lawyer?

You'll find something else to do.

In the meantime, it's not horrible. Every month you send money to pay off the loans – an amount you calculate and recalculate for hours each day while not-working, figuring out exactly how close each month gets you to not-slavery – about five years if you stayed at the firm another five years, but that'll not-happen, so probably fifteen or twenty years in the real world – or at least, that's your best guess. It's not-clear how you're supposed to pay off loans each month if you're not-earning, but for the time being you've decided to not-worry.

One client told me being a lawyer was like being a plumber. Someone has a shitty job and they hire you and you have to do it. So you do it, and you charge them a fortune because no one else wants to do it. And that's that. It's not horrible.

Not-horrible is also getting what you asked for. You did this for the money, remember? The $160k per year? You weren't deaf and blind – you heard the warnings about the hours and the soullessness and all that and you thought – screw it, I can handle this.

Not horrible is limbo. Purgatory. The doldrums.
Not horrible, as one client told me recently, is "meh."
Hey, it's not horrible.

Originally published March 23, 2011.

Maintaining the Alliance

Look around. All you see, probably, is lawyers - lawyers and more lawyers. That's because you spend 90% of your waking hours at a law firm, where that's all there is to see.

At some point in your day, or your week, or maybe your month, you're going to have to see someone who isn't a lawyer - and that person is going to have to put up with you. It may be your spouse, your romantic interest, your buddy from college or a member of your family.

That's your non-lawyer ally. You know deep in your heart it's not a fun job. Whoever he is, he's putting up with a lot – helping you keep it together. To a non-lawyer – a denizen of the real world - the law firm environment can look like something through the looking-glass. To survive behind that looking-glass, you require the assistance of someone from the outside. You can't take this assistance for granted.

One of my clients told me he regrets leaving work every night to grump at his wife. I pointed out that she – his non-lawyer ally - might not be savoring the experience either. But it went further than that. The following week she blew up at him and gave him an earful of what being a non-lawyer ally is like.

Based on that earful – and other earfuls like it - here are a few tips for getting along with your non-lawyer allies:

Just because you hate your job, don't assume she never wants to talk about hers.

Being a lawyer sucks, and your ally hears about it all the time. She's probably committed to memory every detail of what you hate about your job. If she's your life partner, she watches you get up every morning looking like you're marching off for a root canal – then stands back and observes while you storm back at night and either stare into space for hours, or snap and grump and pace like a foul-tempered guard dog.

She's done a lot of listening, and a lot of empathizing. She's tried problem-solving, and realized it doesn't work. She's tried absorbing. She's learned to tolerate being in the room with someone who's frustrated and angry and scared and sad.

How about her?

When my client's wife blew up at him, she reminded him all she ever heard him say about her was that she loved her job – like it was an accusation. And yes, she did love her job, as a professional event planner. But her work could be trying, too, and she had good days and bad days just like anyone else. Sometimes she wished she could come home and find a supportive someone to blow off a little steam with, or bounce an idea off. Instead, she sat waiting - bored and tense and filled with dread - until he stormed in. Then she listened to him grump.

Just because you're living your life on hold, waiting for the end, doesn't mean she never wants to have fun.

You might be committed to a life of suffering right now. Most lawyers are. Maybe you're counting down to the exact moment when you'll have that all-important one year at the firm on your resume so you can flee, or you're senior enough to call a headhunter about an in-house position, or you've paid down your loans to a major milestone, or whatever event occurs in the future that will permit you to live like a human being again. You're hunkered down, holding your breath, waiting for something awful to end.

That's fine. But she wants to go out for dinner once in a while – or see a movie.

Life goes on in the outside, non-law world. People work from nine to five, and then they lead active, healthy private lives that include friends and cultural events and time spent relaxing.

Just because you've decided to say farewell to all that, and pretend it doesn't exist, doesn't mean she's on-board.

A relationship is about positive shared experience. That's basically all a relationship is – time spent together. If there are good times, you grow closer, and more committed to the partnership. If you have bad times, or simply don't see one another, the partnership frays.

You can't take your non-lawyer allies for granted.

I don't have any easy answer to the question, how am I supposed to spend time with my non-lawyer ally when I never leave the office? But there is an unavoidable reality here: if you ignore your non-lawyer allies, they will eventually give up on you.

That means you stop hearing from friends. Even your family members might stop calling, once they've realized they get voicemail and their calls aren't being returned.

It's toughest for a spouse or life-partner. Dating a lawyer can feel like a long-distance relationship – all the disadvantages of commitment, with none of its pleasures. Why make the sacrifice to be faithful to someone when they're never around? You end up doubly alone.

If this column achieves nothing else, let it be an alarm bell reminding you there are people in your life from the world outside law. They might mean a lot to you, and you might be taking them for granted. They can be your allies, and help you survive this. They "get it" - as much as any non-lawyer can - and they may reach out a hand to help. But they're also suffering, thanks to your decision to pursue law – and it's only decent on your part to acknowledge that they're making sacrifices, too.

If they're going to stick around and be there for you, you have to acknowledge their help, and be there for them sometimes. Fair's fair.

Otherwise you could find yourself living a life filled with lawyers, and nothing but lawyers.

No one wants that.

* * *

This post was originally published, in slightly different form, on June 22, 2011, and no, it wasn't greeted by an outcry or rash of comments or flak from readers. Instead there was...silence. Almost perfect silence. In fact, this piece attracted the lowest number of views I'd seen since the early days of the blog.

That's because the original version started with a couple of opening paragraphs drawing a parallel between LGBT people needing non-LGBT allies and lawyers needing non-lawyer allies. It was Gay Pride in New York City that week, gay marriage was on the verge of being legalized in New York State... and maybe I was trying a little too hard to incorporate a queer theme into the column. The analogy was tenuous - it also led to no one bothering to read the piece. I asked two clients what they thought, and they both looked surprised. "Oh – was that your post? I thought that was a gay piece." When they both went back and read it, they said they liked it. One client emailed me later, with the following account of a conversation at her office:

Me: Did you read The People's Therapist post yesterday?

Officemate: No... I didn't see it.

Me: It was the one that seemed to be about gay people.

Officemate: [Laughs] Oh <u>That</u> was it? I didn't know! I didn't read it. I thought it was about gay people.

Anyway, I revised the piece and cut out the gay theme and as a result it's tighter and more readable, if less quirky. I find it ironic that a column chiefly concerned with lawyers' relations with their spouses went unread because everyone thought it was gay. Lesson learned: Stay focused on what lawyers want to read about - themselves.

Not Worth It

I was kidding around with some of the guys at my gym, tossing around the question – would you fight Mike Tyson for $3 million?

One of them joked – I think he heard this on Howard Stern – that he'd fellate Mike Tyson for $3 million. He could spend the first $1 million on mouthwash and retire on the rest.

Then another guy spoke up, a sometime professional heavyweight boxer. (I'm not making this up, he really has boxed, for big money, not too long ago, and has plans to do so again.)

"It's not worth it. Mike would destroy you. There would be no retirement."

He went on to explain what he meant. He knew from experience – this guy had been in the ring. You'd have more than bruises – you'd have concussions, brain injuries, damaged bones and joints. You'd never be the same – and it wouldn't be worth it. You're better off not having $3 million but appreciating the finer things, like being able to walk and talk and think.

I saw his point.

Biglaw is also not worth it, even for big money. That's because it, too, destroys you - just like Iron Mike.

A lawyer client, a fifth year at a big firm on the West Coast, mused to me the other day - "This job wouldn't be so bad if I didn't end up crying alone in my office so much."

"You mean, it wouldn't be so bad if it didn't suck?"

"Yeah," she said. "That's pretty much it. Imagine doing this for ordinary money. No one would consider doing this for ordinary money."

No one would consider fighting Mike Tyson for ordinary money, either. And it's not worth it for $3 million. Big law isn't even worth it for $160k a year. Don't believe it? Allow me to elaborate.

The process begins with sleep deprivation - plain, simple sleep deprivation. Not sleeping. Staying up all night and facing sarcasm if you plan to take the following day off.

One of my clients brought a pillow into work, so she could put her face down on her desk and sleep for an hour at a time. Her officemate saw her, and told her what a good idea it was. Then she brought in a pillow, too. Only at a law firm.

You might not think sleep deprivation is a big deal. Hell, you're a machine. You don't need sleep. All-nighters? No sweat.

Sleep deprivation is like binge drinking. There's a machismo around staying up all night, night after night – like doing ten shots of tequila. You're tough. Not a problem.

Later, as you puke your guts out and pray for sweet release, you realize you were being an idiot.

Read a few scientific studies on sleep deprivation and you will understand it fries your brain and leaves you an emotional wreck. You can't think straight, your immune system crashes, you fall apart. As one of my senior associate clients put it, "I thought I was unflappable when I got here. I'm flapped."

Naturally, if you aren't sleeping, you're also not having a life. So relationships dissolve, friendships fade, your pet starts living with your parents. And you start thinking about boinking that guy from the anti-trust group, even if he isn't much to look at.

Okay. So why is there sleep deprivation at big law firms?

The billable hour, obviously – but also the plain fact that partners and associates are in direct conflict. There is no "team" or "spirit" at big law firms because partners and associates are there to achieve opposing ends. One is there to destroy the other. The other is there to try to survive. It's like Mike Tyson and you in the ring. He seeks to crush you. You cling to life - by trying to focus on the money you're earning.

I had a partner client tell it to my face: "My firm is about partner profits.

That's it, pure and simple."

That's the norm. Partners are in it for the money – just like you. They are under pressure to bring in clients and produce billable hours bearing their name. A partner has no incentive to do law. Once he's landed the fish, he hands the work to associates. Ideally, they slave away day and night, around the clock, including weekends, generating delicious, tasty, yummy, scrumdilly-icious billable hours that funnel easy money into the partner's pocket - and elevate him to star status at the next partners' meeting. The more you work – the more he earns.

Some firms pay lip service to "lifestyle." One senior associate client received a lecture on how she has to get her hours – over 3,000 last year – down to something sensible, like 2,600. Then bonuses came out, and associates who billed over 2,800 got twice the money. If you think this sends a mixed message, you are correct.

The only problem with this marvelous money-making system, according to partners (and yes, they tell me this all the time) – is that associates are incompetent, unmotivated idiots. They aren't meticulous or thorough, and they act like they don't even care half the time. It's a nuisance. You have to double-check everything on Friday and re-double-check it, then send them changes over the weekend so they don't embarrass you in front of the client. You spend half your time cursing them out for being stupid and missing things.

Why are associates such a problem? Because they *don't* care half the time. Why should they? An associate – like a partner – is also in it for the money. And he gets paid whether he works or not.

What, other than money, might make an associate work? There's the occasional crumb of praise - "nice work, kid" - but you don't hear it often and it doesn't mean much coming from the guy who procrastinated until midnight on Sunday to send you the changes to a brief due 9 am Monday morning.

There's the desire to please. That lasts a little while. But again – it's impossible to please people who view you essentially as a commodity. They are pleased when you produce money for them. Then they throw you out and get another associate.

There's bonuses. But lawyer bonuses – even "big" lawyer bonuses - are little more than anemic hand-outs intended to keep you thinking about money instead of contemplating your personal destruction. What law firms refer to as "bonuses" would be considered "tips" in the banking or corporate executive world, where they actually have bonuses – profit-sharing arrangements linked to real achievement that amount to a major portion of their compensation.

There used to be a thing called "making partner." You worked for about 6 or 7 years and did really well and learned a lot and then they anointed you one of them and you made a million dollars. But there are too many lawyers and there's not enough work. They only made more partners when it earned them more money. They aren't making more partners.

The bottom line: Mike Tyson will destroy you in the ring because that's what he does. He's a heavy-weight champion and they destroy people in the ring.

A big law firm is just like Mike: it will destroy you because that's what it does. It is designed to incentivize partners to bring in as much work as possible and to assign as much of that work as possible to stressed associates and work them as hard as possible to make as much money as possible for the partners. That destroys people.

Associates rarely storm out of firms. Like Anne Rice says in one of her vampire novels: Old vampires never die, they're eternal – they fade away. Associates stop trying at some point. You acquire that "marked for death" look – the fatigue, the resignation. You're not even making an effort. You don't even care about reaching the ultimate lawyer dream: paying off the loans and achieving zero net worth. The only priority left at this point is avoiding work, not receiving the dreaded next assignment. You don't wait for the bad review – you long for it. Bring it already. Get it over with.

Law firm money finally stops coming in, and (forgive me one more fantasy novel allusion) - like Gollum losing the One Ring, you will lose the purpose behind your existence. My precioussss!!! And then it's gone....You crawl away, miserable, broken in mind, body and spirit.

Another associate, identical to you in every way, takes your place within hours.

For those who ask me why I'm so angry and bitter and why I think all big law firm lawyers are unhappy and all big law firms bad places – I invite you to take the $3 million challenge. Go ahead - step into the ring with The Baddest

Man on the Planet. Who knows? Maybe you'll be happy there. It might all turn out okay. I might be overly negative. You know – it's only the unhappy lawyers who see The People's Therapist. Self-selection, that's all.

Be my guest. Jump in the ropes and prove me wrong. Maybe Mike's different now. He's vegan. He loves pigeons. It can't be *that* bad. Think what you'll do with all that money...

Originally published April 13, 2011.

PART THREE:

Not Going Out like That
How to Turn this Mess Around

"Three generations of imbeciles are enough."
- Oliver Wendell Holmes

The Nice Ones

I raced downstairs to break the news: I'm leaving. I got a new, non-legal job at a major online book-seller.

The reception at the firm gym wasn't what I expected. My favorite trainer looked pensive, mumbled "good for you, man," then gave me a half-hearted fist bump. The other two trainers, both women, exchanged looks. One grimaced, and quipped to the other, "see, I told you – the nice ones always leave." She caught my glance, and turned serious. "Hey, it's good news. We'll miss you, that's all."

The nice ones always leave.

My client ran into this phenomenon recently. She's a first year, assigned to a major case with two senior associates. The partner's missing in action, so she and the two seniors are running the show.

The good news is the seniors are great guys – and, as a result, she's been one of the few not-unhappy lawyers I've seen all year.

"They're just plain nice," she told me. "The hours suck, the work itself is kind of boring, but nothing's that bad if you're working with people you like. Sometimes we even have fun."

One guy was super thoughtful, and bent over backwards to take time to explain things and create a sense of teamwork. The other was a bit of a kook, with a goofy sense of humor and a light-hearted way of defusing crises.

Then, Monday last week, the firm distributed bonuses. On Tuesday the first senior associate gave his notice. On Wednesday the other said he's leaving, too.

Neither of the seniors said why they were taking off. Maybe it was the demanding, ungrateful client - maybe the partner, who never acknowledged their hard work. Maybe they were just burnt out in general.

As a result of their departure, an office that used to be fun has turned grim. It's like watching a friendly college dorm turn overnight into der Führerbunker. The partner is melting down. He pulled in another senior associate, an anal-retentive who doesn't know what he's doing. People are hiding in their offices. The atmosphere among the paralegals is funereal. Even the contract attorneys look more depressed than usual, if that's possible.

"It's a shit storm," my client said. "And from my perspective, a lose-lose proposition. The partner's overwhelmed, the new senior is clueless and I don't know whether to try to help – and get yelled at – or lay low and hide – and get yelled at."

There's no winning, and it's no fun.

I went through the same thing at Sullivan & Cromwell. The only senior associates I enjoyed working with were Gil Cornblum and one other guy, and they both quit within a few months. (For what happened to Gil after that, read "When the Emptiness Swallows you Whole.") Both times, it profoundly sucked.

The nice ones always leave. That's the general rule.

Sometimes they don't even have to leave – they just fade away. That's what's happened to another client of mine. He's a naturally terrific guy – smart, witty, charming. If he hadn't fallen into law, he'd be a comedy writer (and still might be.) He'll have the whole room cracking up in five minutes flat.

When this guy arrived at his firm, he did what he always does – make friends and entertain people. Everyone knew right away he was one of the nice ones.

This week, he turned a corner.

"I got a call from a partner," he told me. "He said he needed to see me in his office, and I thought, this is it – I'm getting laid off."

Business was slow. He hadn't billed more than 100 hours the last few months. He hated pulling overnighters the first couple years at the firm. Now he was bored and frazzled from the downtime - and waiting for the nudge.

"So I get to the partner's office, and he looks up from his desk and says, 'The firm is distributing bonuses, and you will be receiving x dollars. Congratulations.'

"That was it. All I could think was damn, I thought this would be the nudge – I'd finally be out of there. Then I realized how much I was *hoping* this would be the nudge."

That's when he knew he needed to leave. But his loans are over $100k. He decided to do the slow fade.

"I'm a ghost," he told me. "I barely exist. I used to entertain everyone at lunch, go to the office parties, take the summer associates out – all that stuff. Now I go to the gym at lunchtime, keep my office door closed, and never say anything to anyone. I'm there, but I'm not there."

That's the slow fade.

I remember slowly fading at S&C. I was a lively, amusing presence initially. Then I crashed and turned into a basket case. Finally I pulled back, and started to disappear, until I was barely a presence at all. Then I left.

I watched other "nice ones" go through the process, fading, then departing, one after another.

Those who remained - un-faded and more ubiquitous than before - weren't "the nice ones." They were the lawtistic jerks with chips on their shoulders, the obsessive workaholics, the control freaks, the psycho screamers, the unconscious neurotics broadcasting their misery with sloppy clothes, eccentric personal hygiene or weird physical tics.

The bright, interesting ones? That thoughtful guy you met during the summer program and used to talk books with during the opening months of first year? Long gone.

Then there are the ones who never, ever leave: the deeply un-nice ones. Every firm has at least a few guys like that. They tend to get nicknames. You know, "the beast," "the machine," "the evil" – *that guy*, the guy everyone in the building hates, the one even the paralegals and the secretaries and the librarian and the cleaning staff and the guard downstairs in the lobby hope will somehow *go away*. *That* guy. The one who doesn't merely drink the Kool-ade, he brews it.

That guy will stick around – in fact, he'll make partner. It's as certain as death and taxes. If everyone – every single sane person - is praying to stop it from happening, even the atheists are imploring their higher powers to intercede and foil the *obscenity* of that *creep* making partner... I guarantee you, he's a shoo-in. He'll be managing partner. A name partner. Emeritus partner. A legend at the firm, with a portrait hanging in the reception area. In the distant future, a computer-generated hologram of *that creep* will reach out to shake hands with each and every visitor to the firm each and every day, for all eternity.

The nice ones always leave.

Originally published April 27, 2011.

Maybe You're Not Cut Out for This Place

It seems like the cruelest thing they could say to you, but according to my lawyer clients (and my own experience), they say it all the time:

Maybe you're not cut out for this place.

There are variations, of course. There's the old favorite:

Maybe you're not cut out for this work.

Or – to put the knife in and twist it:

Maybe you're not cut out to be a lawyer.

You've taken the LSAT, applied to law school, borrowed the budget of a small African nation, sat through endless lectures and countless exams, passed the atrocious trivia contest known as the bar, and now you're in a big, powerful law firm... sinking like a stone.

And they're letting you know it's not a fluke, either – it's *you*.

Maybe you're not cut out for this place.

There's always a smug half-smile on the face of the partner who says it, too. Nice of him to tell you now, right?

At least with the "not cut out for this place" line, you can kid yourself life would be better with another employer. There are headhunters lining up to pocket a fee by packing you off to a "lifestyle" firm, where life is sweet and easy.

But you're not that naive. Not after what you've been through. If "lifestyle" firms exist, they are the holy grail of the legal profession – known only to a sacred few, not to every headhunter in the phone book.

The real question is why you run in horror from "maybe you're not cut out for this place," instead of asking yourself whether you really are cut out for this place.

You probably feel that – after all you did to get here – you *have* to be cut out for this place, and you *have* to be cut out for this job. You *have* to be a lawyer because you've sunk too much time and money into it to do anything else. You have no choice, no options, no future.

That's not true.

My lawyer clients often start out sounding that way. I tell them to re-frame each aspect of their lives as a conscious choice. That way you stop being a victim and start taking charge of your own happiness.

Unhappy lawyers tend to give the same reason for why they got into their profession: "I couldn't think of anything else to do."

That's sad. It's also an example of unconscious living – sleep-walking through life. Legal education has become a default path, the easiest thing to do when you don't want to make a decision for yourself. Now that you've trod that well-worn path, the least you can do is re-frame your remaining choices. There might not be easy choices, but there are always choices – even if you have debt.

The first step is to stop doing what you're told all the time. That's how a child lives his life, not an adult.

Maybe you want to leave law completely, and get a fresh start.

You might want to be a chef, or a piano tuner, or open a fashion boutique, or get a job feeding penguins at the zoo. If that's where you want to be, now's the time to get started.

There will be obstacles. You have to prove you want it.

But plenty of lawyers have left big firms and gone on to pursue non-legal careers.

Creating happiness on your own terms is not like signing up for law school. That was easy. Taking charge of your life doesn't require just hard work – it takes imagination. This is not a path for the risk-averse.

The good news is you have no choice. This is not a dress-rehearsal. This is your actual life – the only chance you're going to get to be happy. If you're not happy now, you'd better get on the problem, pronto. Maybe you *aren't* cut out for this place.

Originally published April 7, 2010.

Dancing the Pole

My client's concise estimate of her second year at a big law firm: "Meh."

For months, the "career" consisted of one-third idleness, one-third word-processing, and one-third pointless research. That morphed over time into "managing" doc review, which morphed into *doing* doc review, which translated into odious hours staring at odious documents on a computer and clicking "responsive/relevant" "privileged" or some euphemism for "embarrassing." According to rumors at her firm, there's juicy stuff squirreled away in electronic nooks and crannies – most notoriously, emails from execs hiring hookers. To date, my client's experience of "doing doc review" has matched the edge-of-your-seat excitement of watching drywall compound discharge moisture.

"There are days I want to scream, 'Who are we fooling?!'" she said. "This isn't a career – it isn't even a job. It's a joke. Every day I think about quitting."

But she doesn't. Why?

The $160k per year.

Money changes things. Especially when your school loans top $200k.

Another client, from a while back – an NYU undergrad - was introduced to an older gentleman at a gay bar. This *éminence grise* offered a proposition. A partner at a major law firm, he possessed quantities of money and an apartment on Park Avenue. They devised an *arrangement*. Each week, my client would ride the subway up to Park Avenue, undress in this guy's living room, and, then... *ahem* ..."stimulate himself to climax"in the presence of said partner. Why?

$400 in cash. Usually with a nice tip.

If the partner called, he showed up, no questions asked. You could say there was something in this *arrangement* that piqued my client's entrepreneurial spirit. Or you could say it paid the rent.

Did he feel like a prostitute?

If you work at a large law firm, are you in any position to ask that question?

As The People's Therapist, I've worked with people from all backgrounds and income levels. Yes, I've worked with folks who do sex work - from a woman who monetized the use of her feet for fetish parties, to a dominatrix who did quite well, thank you, spanking older, prosperous suburban gents, to a woman who danced go-go and worked a pole to earn a little cash - to the NYU student who "self-pleasured" in the company of that law partner.

Their response, for the most part, was "meh." It's a job. You show up, do whatever they want you to do – so long as it doesn't violate your comfort zone – and get paid.

Karl Marx compared the bourgeois European wife of his time to a prostitute, because she was exploited as a means of production. She effectively traded her sexual, child-bearing and child-raising services for money, and was exploited by the capitalist as assuredly as one of his workers – or a prostitute.

Many of my big firm lawyer clients aren't sure what they're doing at the office or why they're doing it. You keep showing up in the morning and keep leaving at night. Sometimes you aren't doing much of anything. Other times you're slaving away at a task you half-understand. People keep smiling and saying hello when they pass you in the hall – and that paycheck, the point of the exercise, keeps getting deposited in your bank account. As long as the firm keeps paying - heck, you'll make phone calls, chase down research, prepare a closing table, do doc review... whip quivering buttocks, dance on a pole, or murmur exhortations while your toes are licked. What's the difference? Who cares?

It does raise an issue: Are there lawyers who *aren't* prostitutes?

I never shook off a strong regret surrounding my legal career - that I never learned how to practice law. You know – real law. Like when your friend calls because his cousin got arrested for a DUI. I have no idea what to do with a DUI. I wasn't even a litigator – I was on the corporate side. I wouldn't know where to start.

Here are some other things I know next to nothing about, other than in some vague, theoretical bar exam sense:

How to file for divorce.

How to close on a house.

How to write a will.

How to handle the legal necessities of a small business.

At this point, if a friend rang up with any legal question short of how to prepare for the closing of a multi-million dollar merger - or proof a securities offering – my advice would be useless.

There are lawyers out there who are not proletarian sex workers, right? Lawyers not owned by the capitalists. Lawyers who possess the means of production (as Uncle Karl would say.) Lawyers who crawl out of bondage and ascend to the petite bourgeoisie. Lawyers who "hang a shingle" and do real law. Lawyers who work for themselves.

They probably don't earn much, and face their own struggles. But how glorious it seems! Close your eyes and dream for a moment of holding sole proprietorship of your own outfit, dictating hours, locating clients and cultivating relationships – not meeting a client once at a closing, but knowing that person, as a person, for real, from the start.

No more meaningless human resource fluff about "associate development" and "diversity." You look in the mirror and ask yourself how you did today. No more "pulled into a deal." You eat lunch with a human being and figure out what he needs, then you do it.

I have no idea if this is a Normal Rockwell fantasy hatched by my unconscious. Maybe the last lawyer to operate on those rules was Abraham Lincoln. The reality of working as a solo practitioner could be as exciting and profitable as waiting tables.

But it would be nice, at some level, to know practicing law isn't simply about coming when some oddball partner with an exotic fetish happens to ring you up.

Originally published June 15, 2011.

The Terrible Twos

You pass through a stage when you're about two years old – the famous "terrible twos." It's often marked by stubborn refusals to obey orders, and sometimes downright tantrums. The infant is growing into a person. For the first time, he wants control over his own life.

It's called personal autonomy. You go where you want to go, do what you want to do, and refuse to do what you don't want to do. A crucial phase of human psychological development, it marks the inception of an independent identity, a sense of purpose - and a sense of self.

This week I worked with a young second year from a big firm. She related a hellish story of law firm life.

This past Saturday morning she was at the airport in line with a boarding pass, heading to her best friend's wedding, when her cellphone rang. It was a partner. He needed her in right away.

She explained that she was about to step on a plane.

He asked, "Well, are you actually in the wedding?"

She said no.

"Then you don't have to be there."

You've heard stories like this. One of my clients admitted to a partner that it was actually his step-grandmother's funeral he was leaving the office to attend. This old woman had been married to his grandfather for 30 years and was the only grandmother he'd ever known, but he still lost on a technicality - and couldn't be at that funeral because she wasn't family. Some court filing was more important.

Young attorneys at big firms don't have personal autonomy.

Even for a two-year-old, it is degrading to be treated like an infant. But at least a two-year-old can throw a tantrum. You don't have that option. You have to contain all that anger, and often it gets turned inward, triggering low self-esteem and depression.

You know this problem exists – we all do. The question becomes what to do about it.

I have two suggestions:

First, lawyers can treat one another like adults instead of infants.

Virtually nothing that has to be done by Monday really has to be done by Monday. That is a law firm myth.

I remember, in the business world, my boss demanding that a contract be re-drafted by our outside counsel for Monday morning. It was Friday afternoon. I interrupted the call to say I wanted to take a look at the current draft before then, and that I'd get it to the outside counsel by Monday morning so she could sign off on my changes.

I was lying. But I could almost hear her body collapse in relief. I knew the outside counsel. She was 28 years old and had been planning to go skiing that weekend with her boyfriend. I'd worked as a lawyer at a big law firm and I knew she would be devastated if we trashed her weekend. I also knew it wasn't that important - so I did what I had to.

I approached my boss, a Vice President of Marketing, a few days later, and talked to him about the incident.

"Don't you realize how much they bill us an hour for her time?!" he shouted. "For that money, she should work every weekend."

When money is made more important than people, someone always suffers. I didn't care what they billed us for her hours. I was worried about her. She was a person.

I'm making a plea here for lawyers who have had their weekends ruined to do whatever it takes to make sure someone else's weekend isn't ruined, too.

That means partners can try to make things more transparent, so associates have a heads-up sooner.

That means instead of pulling in some poor junior who's going to his grandmother's funeral, call in a paralegal, who'd probably love the overtime and can do most of the same work anyway.

That means realizing that other people are people, too, and they deserve to have some measure of control over their lives.

My second suggestion is to you lawyers out there whose autonomy is being taken from you.

Don't sink into helplessness and depression. At very least, re-frame this set-up as a choice. You are probably doing this big firm thing for a few years to achieve a goal. Either you want to get senior so you have more say in things, or change firms or go in-house or maybe just pay off the loans and get out of law. This job is a step on the way to somewhere else. Never lose track of that. You have at least that much control.

Take care of yourself, too. Go visit a therapist, and complain a little. It helps to have a place where you're in charge, and can say whatever you want.

You might even stand up a little for yourself at the office.

At the end of my stay at Sullivan & Cromwell, when I already had another job lined up and was about to announce my resignation, I happened to receive "the call" from a partner late on a Friday afternoon. He wanted some document turned around ASAP.

Just for the heck of it, I behaved like a grown-up instead of a frightened child.

"Realistically, Bob, what's the deadline on this?" I asked. "Could I have it for you Monday night or Tuesday morning?"

There was silence for about a count of five. Then he started screaming.

"How about *right now*?! What about you do it *right now*!?"

I answered calmly.

"Okay – not a problem. I just wanted to make sure the timetable was realistic. You see, I had weekend plans."

There was an awkward silence on the other end of the line. He wasn't used to this.

And then I hung up.

It wasn't much. But, like a two-year-old insisting he wanted to walk over there and play with that toy right now, I'd carved out a zone of self-respect.

I'd made a point. I was a person too.

Originally published May 12, 2010 (incidentally, my 44ᵗʰ birthday).

The Calm Center

My tenure at Sullivan & Cromwell ended - along with my legal career - in a smoking crater. Picture scorched earth. Nuclear armageddon. The fat lady sang. (More details to come.)

That said, I actually got off to a pretty good start. At least for the first couple weeks.

I was assigned to a rather jolly partner, a short, roly-poly chap fresh back from running an office in Asia. He didn't seem a bad sort, and I was feeling on top of the world, commencing my career after a month's vacation. Off I scrambled to the library to write a memo on a detail of securities law. The topic was complex, but I kept my cool, summarized what I found - with a touch of wit - and called it a day.

Things went swimmingly. The partner loved the memo. He deemed it clever and refreshing and pretty close to accurate. Apparently, I'd managed to lighten the mood at a key moment in a tough deal. I decided I loved him.

The next week we did the deal closing. As a first year, I arranged for execution of the documents (a trickier proposition in those antediluvian days of fax machines and actual, non-cell, phones.)

To my amazement - remember, I'd been there all of two weeks - the jolly partner had a full-on melt-down the night before closing. I found him pacing back and forth outside the conference room, waving documents and shouting that the senior associate was "going to wreck this deal!"

I hurried over to him – again, I was new, I didn't know any better – and tried to calm him down.

"It's going to be okay," I said. "The senior's a smart guy, and he's doing his best – we're all doing our best. We'll stay focused. The closing will either happen tomorrow or it won't, but it'll happen sooner or later, and everything will be okay."

The partner took a deep breath, and calmed down.

I may have crawled away in disgrace two years later, but that partner at S&C appreciated what I did, and he always liked me. I still think of him fondly.

Why did he like me? Not because I was anything like a competent lawyer. I rarely did more than stand around and send faxes.

He liked me because I kept my cool. I was the calm center.

Sometimes, when the world assumes crisis status, being the calm center gets the job done. Politicians know this. Awful as it sounds, a crisis like 9/11 presents an opportunity to look good. When everyone else is freaking out, you present yourself as the calm center - even if you're not doing anything.

Biglaw attorneys crave a calm center because they face constant crisis. In an ordinary job, if you work a late night or a weekend, it means something major is happening. Afterward, you take a break and recover. But every day is a crisis at a big law firm – and there's no recovery. Even if you are "granted" a vacation, there's the Blackberry – and they won't hesitate to use it.

There's the nature of the work itself, too. Litigation lurches from crisis to crisis – it's a zero-sum game, two combatants fighting to the death, searching for a dirty trick, trying to catch the other out on a technicality. Some of my Canadian lawyer clients tell me it's better north of the border, where people don't bring law suits on a whim, simply to create delay or cost, and lawyers hesitate to torture prisoners and burn villages to the ground. That might sound wussy to an American litigator, but if you're looking for a calm center, maybe Canada's your place.

On the other hand, it's hard to imagine serene, tranquil M&A deals, even in Ottawa.

Towards the end of my time at S&C, when I was too frazzled to form sentences, I managed to locate two calm centers at the firm. I stumbled upon them by accident, but they did wonders towards preserving my sanity.

The first was a trainer at the firm's gym, down in the sub-sub-basement of our building. I'm a fan of physical exercise, and recommend some sort of workout for everyone. But when you're at the bitter end of your time at a law firm, avoiding work and floating in and out of the place like a ghost – the gym is the place to be. You can spend two hours down there at lunchtime, and even the nastiest, most sadistic senior partner, when he comes looking for you, will back off when he hears you're working out. He should be down there too, and he knows it, but he hasn't seen the place in months, if not years. And he's fat. You're untouchable.

I was spending a lot of time down at the gym, and eventually one of the staff walked over, introduced himself, and offered to train me, for free. He wasn't supposed to charge us anyway, and he was looking for something to keep him from losing his mind down there in the sub-sub-basement.

I don't remember his name, but this magnificent man combined the finest qualities of Yoda, Mr. Spock, Merce Cunningham and Lou Ferrigno. He was a chess master and philosophy major, who paid for college with football scholarships - the law firm gig was paying his rent before he started a PhD. Under his supervision, weight-training was transformed into a yogic discipline blended with modern dance. In a matter of weeks I was unrecognizable: I lost thirty-five pounds, and learned the basics of anatomy and movement in the process. His cryptic utterances - "Think from within your body," "surprise the muscle," "start from the core," stay with me a decade later – and I still work out daily with better-than-competent form.

Weight-trainer guru from the S&C gym, wherever you are, thank you. You were my calm center.

There was one other contributor to my not throwing myself off the roof of 125 Broad Street that year – a paralegal from Beijing. I remember he was named Wei Guo, because the lawyers would shout out "wei to guo!" when they saw him in the hallway. It produced no discernible response from Wei, who was more Confucian scholar-prince than S&C paralegal.

Wei was deep. He had that curious Chinese ability to appear profoundly unamused without communicating the slightest disrespect. I can't remember exactly why he was a paralegal at the New York office. He had a wife and small child, and was sent from the Beijing office, probably to perfect his English, which – like most things about Wei – was already immaculate.

In my final year at S&C, I took to eating dinner in the staff dining room instead of the "lawyer's dining room." It was more relaxed – like a college cafeteria instead of the Yale Club. One night I sat across from Wei, hoping to break the ice. He grunted a greeting, then buried himself deeper in a thick, book-like Chinese magazine.

I ate. Wei read. Finally, I dared to ask what the article was about. He froze, then looked up, radiating profound un-amusement. Our eyes met, and he returned to his magazine.

Feeling like I was talking too loud in the Sistine Chapel, I pressed the question:

"C'mon – I'm curious."

He didn't look up again, merely answered in a monotone: "It is a study of the musical debate between the followers of Wagner and Brahms."

I cracked a smile. "Cool."

I'd like to wind up this story by describing how Wei and I became the tightest of friends, etc. etc., but that didn't happen. He continued to look profoundly unamused and kept reading.

Nonetheless, I'd made a friend. Wei was awesome. My hunch was correct – we shared a lot in common. Wei had no interest in S&C or its stupid lawyers (including me) and their nonsensical concerns. He was an intellectual from Beijing University, laying low, posing as a mild-mannered, brusquely competent paralegal - and the whole firm fell for it. That is, except me. I'd found him out. We both knew who Wagner and Brahms were. That was a rare thing at S&C - at least, so far as I could discern from talking to anyone other than Wei Guo.

Thank you, Wei. It was calming, knowing you were there, wandering the beige hallways with those awful hunting prints. You were another subversive element, a center of near-mystical, Eastern serenity, buried deep in the heart of the beast.

Find a calm center. It might preserve your sanity, too.

Originally published March 30, 2011.

You Own This

There comes a time in every big law firm lawyer's career when things take a turn for the deeply serious. After two or three years, someone turns to you and says "okay – you own this," and suddenly you're no longer a glorified secretary or paralegal or guy/gal Friday – you're an actual lawyer.

That's when most Biglaw attorneys think seriously about fleeing for their lives.

For me, the moment of truth arrived after a meeting near the top floor of the skyscraper at 70 Pine Street in Lower Manhattan, one of New York City's iconic spires.

Nowadays we all know AIG as a smoking crater owned by the US government, but back then it felt pretty good to get waived past the guard in their Art Deco lobby, take the special elevator up to the executive suite, stroll into the boardroom, and help myself to a cheese danish.

My job that morning, as I understood it, was to play the part of a little second year along for the ride. I was accompanying an of-counsel from S&C, who actually knew what was going on. I worked hard to look the part, act serious and important and try my best to figure out what they were talking about.

The meeting lasted a couple hours – something to do with deciding on a structure for a deal involving the purchase and simultaneous sale of some smaller companies in the insurance business. The guy doing most of the talking was Howie Smith, AIG's CFO. I smiled and played along.

Afterwards, we admired the view out the window – eighty-five floors up – traded gossip about Hank Greenberg's palatial mansion, and chatted with Howie Smith's son, Mikey, who was visiting the office and wanted to become a lawyer. Then we stepped back into the fancy elevator for the ride back down.

As the doors closed, I felt a chill. The of-counsel handed me a heap of papers.

"Okay, she snapped. "You own this deal."

I gaped at her, uncomprehending. Didn't she realize I was a mere child? A babe in the woods? Totally unprepared for such weighty responsibilities?

"Uh...really?" I sputtered.

She was already gazing at the flashing lights indicating descending floors, unaware of my existence.

That was that. I was screwed.

I had absolutely no idea what I was doing.

It's one thing to be a first or even a second year corporate attorney. Pretty much anyone can handle setting up closing tables and "running changes" and setting up meetings and "taking a stab" at drafting this or that. But then someone turns to you in an Art Deco elevator and hands over the whole mess.

Generally speaking, that's your clue to run for the hills.

I know – you still have loans, and each and every paycheck is one more step towards freedom, but let's get serious – you either are one of those people who can turn into a Biglaw senior associate, or god forbid, a partner – or you're not. You can't fake it – and someone in a position of power is going to figure it out eventually.

I don't know what the precise equivalent of that elevator ride is for litigators. Maybe it's "owning this deposition" or "owning this brief." I honestly have no idea. But you'll know it when you see it. Whatever it is, if you're not really one of them, and you've been faking to get by – well, that's your clue to hit the highway.

Of course, it's always possible you *are* one of them.

I knew a guy at Sullivan & Cromwell, a few years ahead of me, who clearly fit the bill. After our first day working together, it was apparent I was in for hell, but when he didn't seem to need me at 7:30 pm, I slipped out of the office and made it home. I was preparing to walk my dog in a mood of mournful introspection when the phone rang. An icy trickle of sarcasm leaked from the receiver.

Yep, it was him.

"Umm...Will? You comin' back?"

"Right away."

And back I went. We stayed up the entire night while he ran around like a speed freak, mumbling to himself and ordering me to alter documents, print them out and fax the whole mess to Bahrain, London, Beverly Hills, Budapest, Paramus, wherever.

This was a fourth year associate, "running his own deal."

Nowadays this guy's a partner, and from the reports I've received, even at S&C he's considered a little nuts.

For me, that night – and the long unbroken chain of nights like it that followed – drove home the reality I'd never be someone who "ran my own deals."

To become a senior associate, you have to drink a fair amount of Kool-Aid. It means taking the plunge – going in deep, and actually assuming responsibility for very very serious things. You turn into the person who calls terrified first-years and sarcastically tells them to get their asses back in for another all-nighter. You become the person who curses everyone else for being useless and not working hard enough. You become the guy faxing side agreements to Bahrain at 5 a.m.

Eventually, if lightning strikes – at least in the old days when lightning still struck – you turn into the partner who terrorizes everyone around you. You enter the heart of the beast.

But that probably won't happen.

My point is this – at some juncture you realize these people really are big firm lawyers – they're in it for real. You also realize – probably - that you're not.

You don't make partner at a place like S&C just because you're smart and you work hard. You make partner because you're one of those people.

If you're like most of us, you'll know deep down that there's never going to be a day when you are in any way, shape or form prepared to "run your own deal."

That's the moment when you acquire "the stink of death." The stink of death is unmistakeable, cannot be masked by any perfume, and permeates the entire firm. You are marked for slaughter.

I acquired the stink of death at the end of my second year when that lady in the elevator told me I "owned" her deal and we both realized I had no intention of owning anything except my profound desire to get the hell out of Sullivan & Cromwell.

I was in over my head, not so much because I wasn't smart or motivated or whatever. It was mostly a matter of my not giving a damn about that deal, or the firm, or staying up all night, every night, doing something immensely complicated that made my head hurt for clients who, even in those days, seemed as deeply sinister as they were unimaginably rich.

My sole desire at that stage in my legal career – which is to say, riding in that elevator - was to pay off my loans, go home, and play with my dog.

If you want to be the guy who sticks around for years three, four, five, six, seven and on into eternity, you need a little more fire in the belly than that. You might have to be kinda nuts.

Okay – maybe that's unfair. Not all senior associates and partners at big law firms are nuts. But you might as well wrap your head around the reality that you probably will not turn out to be one of those people – and that not being one of those people might not be such a bad thing.

Maybe, like most of us, you'd rather not "own this deal."

You'd rather run for your life.

Originally published December 29, 2010.

I Suck at Law

I uttered those words for the first time over lunch, about six months after I left Sullivan & Cromwell. I wasn't putting myself down. I was setting myself free.

This was transgression - admitting the whole legal "thing" wasn't for me.

It's what you're never supposed to say, because it opens you up for slaughter. It's throwing down your weapon, taking off the armor and walking away from the fight.

Go ahead – tear into me. I double-dare you.

It was a weird lunch. I was sitting with another former associate from S&C. We weren't friends. I actually sort of hated him. For two years he did his best to bad-mouth me and let everyone know he was a better lawyer.

Now he wanted to do lunch.

That's because he'd been laid off (you know, the "bad review" routine.) I'd left S&C and done the impossible – gotten a real job outside law, as a marketing exec.

He said he wanted to discuss "careers outside the law." Yeah. As soon as we sat down he started shooting the shit about our law firm days.

No way.

I felt sorry for him. He had a fiancée and was clearly a mess. But I wasn't about to play along with that bullshit.

I knew what would get his attention. When he paused from the stream of false bonhomie to catch his breath, I seized the opportunity.

"I suck at law."

This produced a deer in the headlights face. I went on.

"I never belonged at that place. Who was I kidding? You were twice the lawyer I was."

From his expression, I'd morphed into a winged goat in a tutu.

First rule at a law firm: Never admit vulnerability. Second rule: Conform. Third rule: Compete.

It felt like an accusation. I meant it that way. You were *much* more lawyer-ey than me. No, really. I *insist*. You were *far and away* the better lawyer. You *are* law, dude. You *much much* law. Me *no* law.

Me free.

No one gave a shit at my new job if I was a good lawyer. That's because I wasn't a lawyer.

I wanted to shout it from the rooftops. Rent a skywriter. Hire a blimp.

From the outside I *look* like a pretty good lawyer. Top 20% at NYU. Article in a journal. Sullivan & Cromwell.

Yeah, well I'm not. I suck at law.

Sorry.

I'm good at school, and law school is school. That doesn't make me a lawyer.

Here are the facts:

I ignore details. I hate small print.

I'm not a "team player." I hate working on stuff with other people.

Money and power bore me. Give me music, books and art.

I'm not confrontational. Put me in a room and we'll all start getting along.

I can't do all-nighters. At 10 pm I go to sleep.

Nothing is more boring than the Supreme Court. They mostly (5-4) hate gay people. I mostly (5-4) hate them.

Litigation terrifies me. It's complicated and scary. Threaten to sue me, and you win. That's it. Take whatever you want and go away.

I suck at law.

The other night one of my clients told his therapy group he was graduating from law school with $200k in debt and no job.

The group – all non-lawyers – stared in horror.

The worst part is he went into the wrong field. After doing some therapy, he sees that he prefers fields like teaching, where he can help people directly.

One member of the group, an immigrant from China, sympathized. He chose to pursue science – neurobiology – because of his limited language skills, but now feels trapped. He loves the humanities and wants to be a journalist in his new language, English.

The law student wasn't Chinese. He was Jewish, from Long Island. There was no good reason why he chose law. When the group asked, he fumbled for an explanation:

"It seemed more impressive than teaching. I wanted money and status."

This guy competed for years, like his life depended on it, to become what a law firm needed - even if it had nothing to do with anything he cared about.

Stop, at some juncture, and ask yourself who you are. Otherwise you end up competing in something you suck at.

You're never going to be good at something if it isn't what you want to do.

At least, I used to believe that, until one of my clients who's a senior partner at a major law firm confessed to me he "hates legal reasoning."

So maybe you can be good at something, even if you hate it.

But you'll still suck at it.

* * *

This piece was originally published on December 15, 2010 and received more reads in a single day than anything I'd posted to date. I guess it struck a nerve. I got a lot of notes saying "yeah, I suck at law too." Doesn't it feel good to admit it?

I Demand the Answer

I receive a steady stream of disaffected lawyers who want to change careers. They come to me for "the answer."

The question is "how do I get out of law and do something different?"

What gets under my skin is the expectation this is going to be easy. It isn't.

Remaining in law and looking for something better poses challenges. You realize by now you can't call a headhunter and go to a "lifestyle firm" - they only exist in the imagination of fee-hungry "staffing professionals." Hyphenated jobs, like "environmental-law" or "entertainment-law" are misnomers. Choose anything fun and attach the word "law" to it - "food-law," "sex-law" - and it's still law. More realistic "remain-in-law" solutions, like an in-house position or a government job, are hard to find because everyone's thought of them. You can get there with sufficient determination – but it's tough and I can't make it not-tough. No one can.

Getting out of law completely poses a new level of challenge - you have to figure out what you truly want to do with your life. I am indeed wise and all-knowing, but I cannot tell you what your purpose is on Earth. This is your journey – and you have to find your own destination. The process isn't like opting for a legal career, where you hop on a train and go where they take you. I cannot talk to you for an hour and concoct some sensible, well-paying, fun, creative job, with status and money, that will make your heart sing and all your problems go away. Remember the last time someone promised that? Look where it got you.

I'm skeptical of "career coaches" and "out-placement counselors," too.

They can help you learn to interview and hone your networking skills – which is useful as you explore options. But you can Myers-Briggs yourself into a coma and still not know your true work. The task is tougher than getting "coached" or "aptitude tested." There is no easy answer. It requires time, and a good deal of soul-searching.

You might need to flounder. That's what people who aren't "K through JD" do during their 20's. As an adult child of the law, you may flounder a little later in the game than everyone else. But if you need to flounder and find yourself, don't pretend it's anything other than that. Saying you've "decided to write" doesn't fool anyone. Taking classes in something creative might be a step on a path forward, but it's only a step. Getting fed up with being a lawyer, and telling everyone you're "writing" is like wandering around a cocktail party after you graduate from college telling people you're working on a novel. Everyone will roll their eyes, and for good reason. They'll assume you're floundering – trying to find a new path. They may or may not respect your struggle, but they'll know you have a ways to go before you can claim a hard-won title of respect, like "writer."

Here's my best advice for what to do if you're a lawyer, hate it and want to do something else:

Probably, you hate it because it isn't taking you anyplace you want to go. And probably, you're terrified of giving up the money.

Pulling the plug on law money is scary. Especially with loans. It can get like crack – you keep promising yourself you'll quit, and then another week goes past, and another. But you know if law is killing you - and if it is, you have no choice: You have to leave. Plenty of lawyers secretly hope to be laid off, just to get it over with.

Once you're off the crack, your primary mission is to figure out who you are. Your authentic identity will pull you to your true work like a lodestone. Meaningful work doesn't just earn money - it expresses your soul.

First – talk to everyone you know, and some people you don't know, about what they do for a living. Don't be afraid to ask questions. Find out how they occupy every day, if they like it, and how they got there. Ask to talk to their colleagues, too. (Yes, this is called networking. It's also called getting to know the world around you – the world outside a law firm.)

Second – make a list of people whose job you wish you had.

Third – do what they did - or whatever it takes - to get a job like theirs.

You might not make it all the way to where they got, but you'll have fun trying.

Be prepared to encounter two new phenomena along the way: poverty and humiliation. Don't worry, they're not that bad, and it's worth it.

People ask me how I stopped being an unhappy associate at Sullivan & Cromwell and transformed miraculously into The People's Therapist.

It took ten years of humiliation, (relative) poverty, hard work and groping in the dark. I stumbled on talents by taking new risks. It wasn't easy. There was a fair amount of crab-walking – not taking a direct path, but stepping in a direction that seemed closer to what I wanted, then turning and doing it again, and again. It's indirect, but it gets you where you're going when you're not entirely sure where that is.

Believe me, when I say I've been there, I don't just mean the hell of Biglaw - I mean the struggle to get out of Biglaw, which was tougher.

Getting the job you truly want – and are good at - requires inspiration, ambition and wanting it more than anything. There's going to be profound, soulful work involved in this process. You will have to listen to your heart, follow it where it takes you, and be who you actually are. This will be the hardest and most satisfying thing you ever did.

That's "the answer." Or the best answer I've got right now.

Originally published March 9, 2011

Don't Forget

My client was sitting at her desk, drafting a complicated, rushed memo. The topic was an obscure derivative. She'd worked all weekend, then come in again early. Her head hurt. It was due at 5 pm. She could barely focus and was feeling panicked. It was 4 pm.

The phone rang. Not thinking, she picked up and barked her last name, sharply, like the partner she worked for did.

"Jones."

It was her ninety-two-year-old grandmother.

"How are you, Sweetheart?"

My client couldn't stop crying.

"All she did was ask how I was," she told me. "That's all it took. I fell apart."

When you enter the world of Biglaw, you pass through a ritual of initiation – LSAT, law school, bar exam, interviews.

Then you enter the bubble.

On the inside, propositions that seem insane in the outside world are taken for granted:

- Two hundred thousand dollars in student loans is within the normal range.
- You have to earn six figures or you are a failure.
- You can't take a vacation just because you "have" a vacation. It must be "convenient."

- Leaving the office at 5 pm shows a serious failure of commitment.
- Taking a weekend off shows a serious failure of commitment.
- Working night and day and doing your best shows a serious failure of commitment.

Last week, another client's mother was rushed to the hospital. He got a call from the emergency room, then sprinted to the train station to buy a ticket home. It was serious – a perforated appendix that could have killed her. He spent the weekend by her side. Once she was back in her own bedroom, recovering, he found himself tucking her plastic hospital id bracelet into his briefcase.

"I know, it sounds crazy, but I didn't think they'd believe me."

"They'd think you were lying about your mother being rushed to the hospital?"

He rolled his eyes. "I know. I know. But they're like that. No one trusts anyone. An excuse to leave for a long weekend? Someone might try it."

The rules are different in the bubble. The worst distortion? Money becomes more important than people.

When my client's ninety-two-year-old grandmother called to ask how she was, it reminded her this old woman is a precious treasure – and she's elderly, and frail. She won't be here forever.

When you work at a law firm, things keep coming up. My client hasn't seen her grandmother in more than a year. That's part of the reason she was crying. The rules inside the bubble take over. You forget who you are. Then an old woman calls and reminds you.

As the author of this column, I'm asked the same question all the time – how do I survive this?

The answer might be: by not forgetting who you are.

That starts with remembering what every child knows: people are more important than money.

My client knew she could concoct some way to take a day off and visit her grandmom. If she had to make up a story, then fine, she'd make one up. Her grandmother was more important than an assignment - or a job, if that's what it came to.

A partner could tell her it's not convenient and she has to cancel.

She could tell the partner sorry, that's not possible.

To keep people more important than money inside the bubble, you have to enforce boundaries. That might be risky, but it's worth it.

The first person worth more than money is you.

I used to take the elevator down from Sullivan & Cromwell once in a while. To the ground level. Then I'd go outside.

I looked at trees. That's it. To remind myself they exist.

It's just a job.

Trees matter. Nature matters. Art matters. Friends matter.

If things get that bad at a firm, you can leave. To hell with loans and "career" and all that. If this place is killing you, you can depart. You are more important than any other consideration. If this environment is toxic for you, you need to get out.

People matter. You matter.

If you're going to enter the world of Biglaw, remember what it is, a bubble.

Don't forget to visit your grandmother.

Originally published February 23, 2011.

You do Law. No, YOU do Law.

My client is in the horns of an uncomfortable dilemma.

Here's the scenario:

He and his wife are both in law, and both want out. Resources exist to permit one to escape. The other must remain behind to pay loans.

Who makes it to freedom? Who gets left behind?

Arriving at that decision can wreak hell on a marriage.

A successful partnership requires an alliance, which depends upon shared goals. If the primary shared goal was being wealthy, powerful lawyers, and that goal cartwheels in flames into the tarmac at three hundred feet per second... the alliance fractures. Sometimes the alliance transforms into opposition.

You do law. No, YOU do law.

That kind of opposition.

My client met his wife at a first-tier law school. They were in the same class, and their shared dream was simple – they would graduate at the top of their class, join powerful, big-name law firms, and make a lot of money. They would have a nice house, maybe a couple of kids, fabulous vacations – and a kitchen with granite counter-tops and an AGA stove.

This was a simple, bourgeois dream – stability, money, family. Naturally, they were intellectuals, so they'd have a subscription to the local symphony – but their dream was about making it, in predictable, concrete terms.

Then reality hit.

They hated their firms. He got laid off, which came as a relief. She went in-house, and to her surprise, hated it even more than the firm. She ended up quitting.

They relocated to another city, where he found a job at a smaller firm. He hates it less, but still basically hates it. She's still out of work, dragging her feet. He's paying both their loans every month – and resenting it.

She says she can't do law anymore – it would crush her soul. She needs to go to grad school and study art or she'll go crazy.

He wants to go to grad school and study history – or he'll go crazy.

They both think the other should stay and do law to pay the bills.

Remember the old shared goal? Charred embers. There are new goals - and they're no longer mutual.

When he's not slaving at the firm, they're fighting. That's driving them both nuts.

Her argument is simple: she cannot do law. She hates it. She refuses to consider it. If she can't go to graduate school, she's heading home to her family. Alone.

To him, time at a law firm represents a waste of his life. He's willing to pay off his own debt, but there's no way he's going to tackle hers.

He has a point. It's unfair to expect him to pay her loans. He could maintain his own loans and get on with his life, escaping to do something with meaning. He's talking divorce.

I'm sympathetic to her desperation, too. She's not my client, so I haven't heard her side of the story, but according to him, she hates their shabby apartment in the new city where they're living. And with school loans, they can barely afford that place.

These two need to get their work lives sorted or they'll never work as a partnership again. That means they need some new, mutual goals.

There are three aspects to life – playing, working and loving – and they must be tackled in order. If you don't have working down, you're entering a partnership with unfinished business that will cripple things up.

Your work tells you who you are – it represents what you create during your life, and it provides you with confidence that you contribute something valuable to the world around you.

This couple has no authentic work – so they are flailing, groping for an identity. Until they discover the answer to who they are, they won't know their work, and they won't know each other.

Even if I were seeing this couple as a couple, and not merely serving as the individual therapist for one partner, it would not be my job to keep them together. I show them what they have – where they want to go from there is their business. This partnership might need to come apart, so they can go their own ways and find their own work. Once that undertaking is accomplished, they could find the confidence to support a new partnership.

Trying to make your partner give up his search for who he is so you can follow your own muse is a recipe for disaster. There will be resentment. The partnership will fall out of balance. One partner will be problematized (she needs to find herself) – the other will over-produce to compensate (he's working to pay off both their loans.) The alliance will erode.

It's not enough to make the other person "do law."

You each have to find your own way out.

Originally published February 2, 2011.

I ♥ Law!

I feel self-conscious sometimes about my deep pessimism with regard to law as a career path. That pessimism reflects what I see every day in my practice – miserable lawyers.

My experiences might be skewed as a result of self-selection. It makes sense that unhappy lawyers would seek a psychotherapist who is a former lawyer and writes a column like mine, and it makes sense that these same unhappy lawyers would write me letters and post comments on my site about their (mostly unhappy) experiences.

Also, in fairness, the country is in the midst of a deep recession. It's hard to be happy at any career when you can't find a job, or half the offices on your floor are empty and there isn't enough work to go around and you're worrying about whether you'll have a job next week. I see clients from other industries who are also affected by the economic downturn, such as folks in the fashion and retail world, many of whom are struggling with long-term unemployment, and even bankruptcy and foreclosure. They're not exactly brimming with high spirited fun either.

The difference is that those people love what they do. They're just out of work.

With lawyers, even the ones who have well-paid jobs seem – mostly - unhappy.

Nevertheless, in keeping with this week's theme of cheerful good times, we're going to ignore them – and talk about happy lawyers. Bouncy, perky, downright merry, good-time lawyers.

I have seen a few happy lawyers. They exist, and they tend to fall into two groups.

The first group work in criminal law. I've met prosecutors, attorneys who specialize in indigent defense, and even some lawyers doing white collar defense, who are happy in their careers. These are the guys who grew up wanting to be Atticus Finch or Perry Mason. They typically love their jobs, and are proud of what they do. Some indigent defense lawyers have described their careers to me as a calling – they are deeply committed to their vital role in our society.

The other happy lawyers are the guys with lifestyle jobs – the ones who work normal hours, report to reasonable, supportive supervisors, and generally don't mind being lawyers. Some quirky small practices fall into this "lifestyle" category. I've run into lawyers who specialize in employment contracts for fashion designers, run a "beverage and alcohol" group at a smallish west coast firm, or handle bi-lingual business for Chilean corporations operating in the US. It's not so much about the work, but the laid-back, supportive atmosphere of these places. Going off the beaten path tends to let people relax - maybe because there's less competition. I've seen a similar effect with lawyers who work in federal agencies and sometimes in-house counsel jobs, where – at least compared to big firms - the culture is friendly, the hours reasonable and the supervisors supportive.

Those two groups are the happy lawyers. They love the law, or at least don't especially mind it.

The rest of the attorneys I treat – the vast majority – not so much.

So...what are the lessons to be learned from observing happy lawyers? Here are some big ones:

You must escape the "billable" hour. Neither of the happy groups was obsessed with the "billable hour." They don't make a lot of money, so they can relax, and concentrate on the work.

Criminal lawyers often sincerely care about their clients, whether they are protecting an indigent defendant's civil rights, or assisting law enforcement by prosecuting a criminal. This is important work, and it means something to them beyond a paycheck.

The lifestyle lawyers might not be quite so inspired, but they enjoy a pleasant environment with colleagues who respect and appreciate them.

One requirement for happiness, law-wise, is not working late or on weekends. It's that simple. You need a life. A little fun with your colleagues helps, too. A bi-lingual lawyer from the Chilean-American firm told me the folks in his office get together for tapas and sangria every week. There's no pressure to attend – it's just a chance to unwind with friends and share a laugh. If you work at a big law firm, that might sound like an opium dream – but it exists. Remember, in the non-law world, colleagues become friendly and go out for dinner and drinks all the time. And they leave work at five. And no one yells at them. Really.

You must enjoy law. If you don't like legal work, you're not going to be happy doing it every day. That should be a no-brainer, but many people, when they go to law school, have no concept of what practicing law means, and you can't acquire that knowledge by sitting in lectures or memorizing doctrine for exams. Plenty of law students talk about enjoying law school, or "learning to think like a lawyer" – but few know if they really – honestly – enjoy the day-to-day work that lawyers do. It isn't for everyone. Some unhappy lawyers simply hate the work. It is detail-driven and if you're not the type, can bore you to tears.

The criminal lawyers I've met usually enjoy the combative, exciting work of negotiating pleas and making a case in court. The happy lifestyle lawyers typically don't mind the work they're doing or actually like it.

In fairness, it's tough sometimes to tell whether it's the work that's the problem. It's easy to get caught up in the intellectual excitement of drafting a complex brief or memo, or preparing for a tense deposition, or sitting in the midst of a negotiation with millions of dollars hanging in the balance. Even doc review isn't so bad if there's a friendly atmosphere and interesting people to work with. But even interesting work stops being enjoyable when you put in eighty hour weeks, sacrifice your social life and receive little or no appreciation for your skill or dedication.

Don't compete with the pack – go your own way. Law can be endlessly competitive, and it's easy to get caught up in fighting for that big law firm position and lose track of your own priorities. Most criminal law folks go their own way early on. They might be in the minority at the top law schools, but if that's where your heart leads you, follow your gut – you might find happiness.

If you're looking for a lifestyle job, it's better to start early, too, since they're hard to find. If you want a specialized boutique, or an in-house job in a particular industry, or a federal agency that concentrates in one area of law, do whatever you can now to tailor your resume to their needs.

Summary: Two big lessons – know yourself, and take care of yourself.

You should be in law because it speaks to who you are, and you honestly enjoy some aspect of the work lawyers do. Pursuing money or prestige isn't going to make you happy. You must enjoy what you're doing every day.

The second lesson is equally important. Even if you're doing work you enjoy, you must make sure you are being treated well.

Yes, happy lawyers exist. If they seem the exception to the rule, it only highlights the challenges that lie ahead for anyone entering the legal field.

Know yourself. Take care of yourself.

Not exactly a startling directive to come from a psychotherapist - we're all about awareness and self-care.

But for lawyers, this seems like important, and overdue advice. Heed it – and you might be one of the happy ones.

* * *

This piece first ran on June 23, 2010. Some lawyers wrote in to correct my theory that the only happy lawyers are either in criminal law or some sort of "lifestyle" job. They said the real trick was working for the public good. On the other hand, I worked as a summer intern at the ACLU after my first year of law school, and saw plenty of miserable lawyers in a non-profit environment. Others wrote in arguing that criminal defense attorneys doing white-collar defense at big firms are just as miserable as any other big firm lawyers. Since some of the comment-writers were doing white-collar defense work at big firms, they might have a point. I guess the secret is to do criminal law that helps someone who really needs it – not just for the money. Or to work at a not-for-profit that encourages a supportive, healthy lifestyle. It still boils down to knowing yourself – and taking care of yourself.

Stooping to Conquer

It's frustrating, trying to teach lawyers the fundamentals of doing business. Several of them arrive in my office each month, seeking advice on changing careers - but they haven't got a clue.

That's because they still think success is making your parents happy. Lawyers start out as the kids who do everything right. They behave. They obey. They get good grades. Typically they aren't especially talented at anything – just good at everything. The formal education system is designed to reward that sort of bland "goodness." It isn't about getting an A in any one subject – it's about getting "all A's."

That doesn't make any sense in the real world. You don't need all-A's, you need to discover the work that you love to do.

A friend of mine at Harvard failed or nearly failed half his courses every year. His grade-point average was dismal. Why? He was in a laboratory day and night, doing PhD level, cutting-edge biochemical research. He used to laugh at the academic advisors who lectured him about his grades. Now, after a successful career as a scientific researcher and inventor, he's become a millionaire venture capitalist. He knew what he wanted to do - and wasn't going to let his GPA hold him back.

A lawyer would never take that path – in fact, he couldn't. Legal education is all about exams, exams and more exams, and being the very best on every one, even if only by a tiny percentage. From that one extra point on the LSAT to that one extra point on the bar exam, it's about everyone doing the same thing, but beating the next guy by a hair.

With that training, you end up utterly unequipped for the world of business, which is why the transition to business is so difficult for a lawyer.

Legal education, and law firm work, is infantilizing. It regresses you into the child who instinctively desires to delight a parent. You try to please an authority figure by doing what they say. You do the work, and make them happy.

That strategy is doom for an entrepreneur. To succeed in business you must separate from the parent, and begin to parent yourself. That means letting go of pleasing others, and becoming the authority figure in your own world. You're the boss. You follow your own instincts. You make yourself happy.

Here are some rules for stamping out the lawyer in you and embracing the business person:

Develop people skills.

A young lawyer client asked me to help him get out of law, and I suggested group therapy, so he could work on his interpersonal communication. He nixed that idea, saying it wouldn't be a good idea for him, since he "tends to shut down in groups."

If you are trying to do business, you can't "shut down in groups" - you have to "light up" in groups. Business isn't about disappearing into your office and working all night. It's about networking, exploiting contacts and getting people excited about you and what you're selling. Which brings me to another rule...

Learn to sell.

Another lawyer client said she was unhappy with the legal profession and wanted to make the jump to business. I suggested she get her foot in the door with a sales position. She made a face. "I could never sell," she explained, and from her expression she obviously considered the task beneath her. Perhaps she had visions of door-to-door vacuum cleaner salesmen, people cold-calling for life insurance companies, that sort of thing. She wasn't prepared to stoop so low.

It's time to start stooping. Everything about business is selling. It doesn't have to be vacuum cleaners or life insurance. Across the board, someone has to bring in the business. Even in the legal world, a partner who can bring in clients takes home ten times what anyone else earns - and spends his afternoons on the golf course. He doesn't have to do legal work – any idiot can do that. He's handling the hard part: selling.

If you're going to sell effectively, you have to remember: **Don't do what you're told – do what your gut tells you.**

Ten years ago, I was confidently assured by other attorneys that I could never work outside law. It was too late for me. With a legal resume, no one would hire me for a business job.

A year later, they were taking me out to lunch, asking me how I did it.

The first step was to stop listening to other people telling me what I could or could not do.

That starts with: **Don't be a lawyer – be a business person with a law degree.**

You have a law degree. That's all they need to know. Meanwhile, play up everything else you've ever done – the original stuff, the stuff everyone else hasn't done. Your identity is something you decide – it's not decided by your resume.

And don't forget: **Take risks.**

It drove me crazy, in the business world, having a lawyer in the room when I was trying to close a deal. I'd work for weeks, schmoozing and negotiating, until we were inches away from payday. All the lawyer had to do was write up a contract and help me get it signed...but he never did. Instead, he would attack the other side like a pit bull over some nonsense in the boilerplate – potentially sabotaging the bigger picture, which was the healthy working relationship I'd built up with these people I was looking forward to working with, as business partners, for years to come.

Lawyers always feel they have to prove their worth by warning you of risks and clumsily trying to off-load that risk on the other side.

I knew about the risks. The other side did too. You take risks in business. That's how you make money. Successful business people don't rack up "billable hours" avoiding risk at any cost. They assume the risk of trusting someone else and working together to create a successful business – selling a product someone out there wants and needs.

How's that for un-lawyerly thinking?

Originally published May 19, 2010.

All that Money

I've been struck of late by how many senior associates tell me they're investing in real estate – not fancy homes or deluxe apartments, but humble, multi-family units in middle class neighborhoods, places where the landlord lives upstairs and if the plumbing stops up, you go knock on his door.

For the record, most young lawyers don't have the luxury of buying anything right now - they're up to their ears in school loans. Only a lucky few have managed to stick with brutal Biglaw jobs for seven or eight years and pay off their loans. These long-term survivors have reached that point where, in the old days, they'd be aiming for partnership - but many of them are no longer eyeing that route. Instead, they're planning for something closer to a modest retirement.

The dream has shifted. Instead of kissing up to law firm rainmakers and scaling the heights of Mount Olympus, many senior associates are settling for a semi-detached house in Queens that generates rental income sufficient to cover the mortgage.

Why the change in aspirations? For starters, let's take a look at partnership – and what it actually means.

The ceremonies of partnership have mutated into a cliché. We all know the routine. You make partner, celebrate over champagne, and the world is your oyster. You are a super-lawyer, assuming your rightful place among the towering legal minds of your generation (cue theme song from "Lifestyles of the Rich and Famous.")

First, you buy a house in Scarsdale - or a Park Avenue apartment.

Then you buy a vacation home in the Hamptons (or a farmhouse upstate), and produce two (or probably three) children, who attend private school and posh summer camp.

When the first kid hits junior high, you divorce wife #1, give her the house and a lot of money and find a cute young blonde to marry as wife #2, buy another house, and produce at least one more child, with the usual *accoutrements*.

Your mid-life crisis – the *major* mid-life crisis - coincides with an affair with a young associate at the office. You divorce wife #2, pay her alimony, and pick up the cost for her rehab from a prescription pill habit.

You buy an ultra-chic TriBeCa bachelor pad, an elaborate stereo system and a piece of art by Andy Warhol.

Your connoisseurship for fine single malt scotch mutates into a dependency on fine single malt scotch.

Things don't work out with the young associate, or the next young associate. You buy a Porsche.

One day you find yourself seated in that Porsche, idling in heavy traffic, gazing up at the bumper of an SUV.

You have arrived. You are living the dream.

That's partnership. Go ahead, admit it, you crave this – the money, the status, the glamor. It speaks to your soul.

The problem is – even if you do believe in this scenario, and actually desire it - partnership doesn't happen very often, not anymore. And when it does, firms aren't looking for partners with good taste – they want partners who taste good. At some point even the dimmest senior associate realizes making partner is no longer about writing killer briefs, or inventively structuring deals – it's about bringing in customers. That boils down to who you know – and how good you are at schmoozing.

My client, a senior associate at a big firm in New York City, works for a partner who doesn't even appear to be a lawyer. This partner is married to an heiress – the daughter of an industrial magnate. The only "work" he performs each week consists of working her rolodex – and his buddy network from Hotchkiss – and bringing in business.

He looks the part – six foot one, perfect hair, expensive suits. There's a posh apartment on the Upper East Side, and a summer place on one of those private islands on Long Island Sound that no one's ever heard of unless they're totally loaded.

His job is to bring in work, dump it on my poor client, and forget about it. Occasionally, if he's meeting one of his clients at the Oak Room for martinis, he'll ask for "an update" on a deal. My client receives an email on his Blackberry with the name of the deal on the subject line. The body of the email is simply a question mark: "?"

Firms need overpaid schmoozers like this guy. They bring in the business that makes everything else happen.

Any overworked drone can do the law part. That's easy. It's hooking the clients that counts. Partners without connections, who don't bring in business, are barely worth mentioning – pitiful, under-paid creatures who cringe in their offices doing other partners' work. These "service partners" get fired all the time (yes, partners do get fired.) In reality, they're no better than senior associates. Slavery is slavery.

If true partnership isn't going to happen – and any other kind of partnership doesn't look so great - well, what then? Your debts are paid off. Why are you still there?

Probably, because you're scared of the outside world. By this point you're like one of those abused animals who, when you open the cage, is too terrified to leave.

It's a scary world out there, outside the law firm. Imagine not having a job – not having a pay check. Imagine walking around, on the outside, not knowing what you're going to do next. Imagine having to find a job – without a job. That's forbidden! You're not supposed to have even *one week* on your resume that isn't fully explained, covered in approvals and signed by the custom's officer, vetted and cleared and absolutely positively not suggestive of the nightmare - Unexplained absence! Flakiness!

At very least, you doubt – with some reason – that you'll ever be able to make this kind of money doing anything else.

So you stay. And you work. And you hate it.

The question becomes: If you're going to stick around and work that job

- what do you do with the money? You can waste it – blow it on endless Louis Vuitton bags (I met a lawyer who blew quite a chunk that way) or clothes or fancy restaurants, or an expensive rental apartment you don't really need or wherever money goes when you waste it.

Or you can put the pieces together – and use that money to subvert the system.

You can work for yourself. One of my clients is saving up to buy a bar – a neighborhood dive with a jukebox. That's his dream – and it might pay for itself, too.

But the easiest way to work for yourself? Become a landlord.

Once you've decided to go off on your own – to plan your own future - the firm becomes little more than a source of cash flow. They provide the cash (at least for the time being) and you invest it. That's subversive because you're no longer there to please - you're there to exploit. Just like they exploit you.

Take their money. Buy an investment property. Pay down the mortgage. Buy another. Eventually the cash flow from tenants might become enough – you won't need the cash flow from law. If you do, you can open your own law office and get your own clients. You can put your office in your own building.

That's when you're free.

One of my clients is the master of this approach. She snickers if you talk about making partner – she could care less. She's a sixth year, and an excellent lawyer. She cranks out work, and she cranks out good work. She's a law firm's dream – the mid-level associate you can count on. Partners fight to get her on their deals.

But she's not in it for them – and she doesn't want to become them. Her loans were minimal (thanks, Mom and Dad) and she's been scrimping and saving for a long time, funneling every cent into modest, but profitable investment properties. Her new project is a friend's microbrewery, in which she's become a partner and legal advisor. In a few years, according to her projections, she'll own several modest properties, along with the rental income. By then the brewery is projected to go profitable – and she'll be a shareholder.

She seems to know what she's doing – and she's doing it for herself. The person she's working to please is the same person she stares at in the mirror.

She's not the only one. There's a change in the air.

Associates are doin' it for themselves.

Go Climb a Mountain

My client was telling me about his new job.

On the face of things, there was nothing to complain about. He'd hated his old firm — a Biglaw institution he called "soulless." The new place, a New York City-based securities boutique, was different. The people were smart – practically cosmopolitan by comparison. And for the first time, he wasn't being treated like a junior. They respected his judgment – no one was correcting his work.

I offered congratulations.

He looked thoughtful, and I asked what was wrong.

"This is going to sound crazy."

"Crazy is my business. Try me."

"I didn't want to get this job. I was hoping the old place would fire me."

"Okay. Why?"

"I wanted to be free."

He'd gone so far in pursuit of his secret fantasy of getting fired that he'd planned a trip to India and investigated moving to Oregon, where an old friend lives. He had money saved up, and was ready to apply for unemployment and sell his apartment. It was all worked out. He was going to escape – to chase a dream of living near the mountains and surrounding himself with laid-back, creative people.

Now – by a stroke of luck – he was sitting in another big city law firm, earning a hefty salary, continuing with his career.

He had nothing to complain about – but he was crushed.

The problem was simple. He was going nowhere – or, at least, nowhere he wanted to be.

This guy could stick around at this firm for twenty years and end up a senior securities attorney – maybe even a partner. He'd be wealthy. He'd attend bar association thingamabobs and sit on panels. He'd have his own clients and bring in business. That was where he was headed if he stayed on his current track, passively charting the course of least resistance.

But he didn't want any of that. He didn't like securities law. He didn't really like law, period. He just fell into it because he needed something to do, and stayed for the money.

He sat in my office, talking about what might have been.

"My friend owns a restaurant in Oregon, on an old wharf. They specialize in organic, locally-grown food. I was going to move to Oregon and manage the place for him. I wouldn't earn much, but my friend says I have the personality and the talent to run a restaurant. And I love Oregon – living near the forest and the sea."

I asked him what was stopping him from quitting right now to pursue his dream.

"I'd never have the balls. I couldn't give up this money."

"Not even for your dream?"

He shook his head. That was that. It was decided.

Stasis is a trap between anger and fear. Anger that you aren't living the life you want. Fear that if you let go, you'll lose everything.

I'm sure you have your own problems. You might not feel sorry for a guy earning over $200k at a top firm. Fair enough. But whatever this guy was earning, his misery was genuine, and I see people like him all the time, trapped in a dead end because they cling to stability instead of chasing a dream.

Stability is a pointless goal. It's a myth. There is no stability in this world. The child in you longs for stability because children are helpless, vulnerable creatures. But you're not a child anymore, you're an adult. You don't need to spend your entire life worrying about your retirement savings. People manage, somehow. They just do. If you're doing something you love, you'll do fine. You're going to die anyway, rich or poor.

The real point of living – adult living – is to chase a dream. That's how humans work. You need to chase something you truly desire, or you'll never feel fulfilled.

If your dream is making it to the top at the legal profession, and that's the path you're on, good for you.

But if you're only in this field because of the money, or because you're too scared to follow your dreams – it might be time to break the stasis, overcome your fear, and try something new.

Life is a brief opportunity for joy. It's about chasing a dream, and it should be exciting and risky and surprising. Somewhere off in the distance, there's a place you want to be – a mountaintop you want to climb. You have a short time in which to race off and see if you can get there.

Go ahead. Break free and chase your dream.

Otherwise you're going nowhere – at least, nowhere you want to be.

* * *

This piece originally ran on June 16, 2010 and triggered a long string of comments - it clearly struck a nerve with my readers. It was loosely based on an actual client's experiences, but – to protect anonymity – I changed all the details. As I dreamt up a new set of specifics for this guy, I realized something important: the particular facts in this column were beside the point. Whether it was a he or a she, a real estate lawyer or an IP litigator or a tax specialist, who wanted to move to Oregon or New Hampshire or Texas, and open a restaurant or a hair salon or a pet shop, didn't matter. What mattered was the message – that to be happy, you need to have a dream, to be going someplace you want to be. That message is universal, and absolutely essential - and it resonated strongly, making this one of my most popular posts to date.

PART FOUR:

My Role in All This

The Annals of Lameness

Just for fun, I asked my client for the single lamest reason she ever gave for going to law school.

She blushed. "Don't make me say it."

"C'mon. It's just us. I'll never tell. Was the Constitution a living, breathing document? Did you want to learn to think like a lawyer?"

"God, no. I wasn't that far gone."

"Then what?"

"I can't believe I'm telling you this. Okay, here goes." Deep breath. "I told people: 'I love to argue.'"

"You are so kidding me."

"I am so humiliated. And now I have to go back to the office."

"Oh, it'll be great. Just imagine - maybe you'll get to *argue*. And *to think like a lawyer* about the *living, breathing Constitution*. Maybe you'll get to argue *and* think like a lawyer about the living, breathing Constitution *at the same time*!"

"Maybe I'll get to stay up all night managing doc review so I can pay off loans and quit."

And so The Annals of Lameness were born, in which the lamest aspects of law are, once annually (or at least, once so far...) gathered together and celebrated. I contemplated an awards ceremony, with categories and winners and runners-up...but I'm too lazy, so I'll freestyle it, which means, make it up as I go.

Second runner-up for the lamest reason given for becoming a lawyer: "I want to help people."

Yeah. That's why you went into commercial litigation.

Drum roll, please.

In the category of: worst experience at a law firm (overnight)...

Oh, to heck with it. I'll tell my story, from Sullivan & Cromwell. You all have your own. We all have our own.

I'm sitting, with fabulous friends, Saturday night, at 9 pm, dressed for a night out, at a nightclub theater type place in the East Village. Kiki and Herb start their act. Kiki delivers one of her best lines: "Ladies and Gentlemen, they say - if life gives you lemons, made lemonade. (Meaningful pause.) Well, Ladies and Gentlemen, life gave me shit."

As if on cue, my cellphone buzzes (this is pre-Blackberry.) The waitress is bringing our green appletinis.

I step outside. It's a senior associate. "Where the fuck are you! You need to be at the printer NOW."

I return to the table, and mumble an explanation to my friends. They exchange looks.

(Okay, after writing this section, I realize this wasn't just pre-Blackberry, it was *pre-cellphone.* Which means I must have done what I now recall doing in those days, which was calling in to an answering machine at Sullivan & Cromwell every 4 hours – that was the rule. Which means – *yes* – I ran out to find a *pay phone*, dropped a quarter in, dialed, got the message from the senior, returned to the club to make my apologies, then rushed out again. Wow... even lamer.)

Back to our narrative.

I arrive, breathless, at Bowne Legal Printers in TriBeCa, still in my going-out clothes. I feel ridiculous, but no one seems to notice. It's a shelf take-down – corporate debt. I'm a first year. I don't even remember being assigned to it.

There's a partner I don't recognize. He leaves as I arrive. There's the single worst senior associate ever, the fat guy with unkempt hair who doesn't cut his fingernails. That guy. He glowers. I'm in trouble.

My job is to sit there all night, waiting for proofs of a red herring or tombstone or offering circular or prospectus or whatever the hell it is. I have to "proof" it, he explains. That means running my fingers down the beginnings and ends of the sentences in the draft and the proof to make sure they match. The printers sometimes drop a line of text. That would be an unimaginable disaster.

I sit and wait. The senior goes home. I'm there alone - in my going-out clothes. It's 2 am. It's 4 am. It's 6 am. I am in hell. I'm not even sure what I'm doing. Just waiting. I try to sleep, but they only have chairs, no sofa, so I'm scrunched up in one, groggy and turning over and over, when the senior associate returns. He glowers.

The proofs arrive. They look fine. We go home, with orders to meet back at the office in two hours.

This story is so lame you can make up the rest. Back at the office another deal explodes. Another partner, another senior associate and another all-nighter. Whatever.

The annals of lameness.

New category: Most pointless assignment (involving travel)

First prize: You fly all the way to Seattle, business class, with a paralegal and an of-counsel, to do due diligence for a client who might purchase a company. You get there, check into a fancy hotel, get driven out in a van to company headquarters and go to the document room. There are only five boxes. Three are nearly empty. You have two people and two full days set aside to look at practically nothing. The of-counsel takes you aside and tells you to look busy, make a list of everything, whatever – just look busy. So you create a spreadsheet, listing each document and everything you can think of to say about it:

"A lease. Dated March 12, 1999. In Japanese. Apparently for real estate."

"Purchase receipt. For 'Lubricating Fluid'. Dated July 18, 1997."

"Receipt for parking services. Dated January 1996. ParkRite Services, Tacoma, WA. $1,035."

You're not even sure what you're looking at. You're making a fair amount of it up. Two days, eight hours each day, of inventing a spreadsheet of minutiae. You get the evening off and take the paralegal out for a "fresh-caught King Salmon" dinner at the top of the Space Needle, which is actually kind of nice.

Back in NYC, the of-counsel tells you the deal fell through – our client was out-bid. But they appreciated the great job you did on that spreadsheet. This is the one and only time anything you ever did made her happy.

We're on a roll here...

Next category: Most humiliating moment at a law firm.

First prize: There was an associate at S&C when I was there named Jorge, who was the first-born scion of the managing partner of the top law firm in Chile. In fact, Jorge's father appeared to own South America. Jorge was sent to S&C on a purely diplomatic mission - the Chilean crown prince spending a year hunting on the lands of a neighboring kingdom.

Jorge was my officemate for a few months. He wasn't a bad guy - but those were exquisitely humiliating months, especially when senior partners would casually drop in, like it was no big deal.

It went a little like this: The partner in charge of structured finance (or whatever) "pops by" our office to say hi, like that was normal, like he was the friendly resident adviser in a college dorm. I look up from my computer, where I'm "running changes in a document" (i.e., glorified word-processing.) The partner doesn't notice me - he steers a course to Jorge's desk, and slaps a broad hand on his shoulder:

"Jorge – glad you could join us at the opera last night. Everything going okay? Great. Nice to see you've settled in. Listen, my wife and I – and a couple of the other partners and their families – are flying to Martha's Vineyard over the weekend and I hope you'll join us. Nothing but golf and a bit of relaxation. I sent an invitation to your wife, but I wanted to make sure to ask you myself. Sound good? Terrific. Okay – you take care and we'll see you soon."

He turns to leave, then hesitates - an afterthought. There was something else...oh, yes - that other living being, the sub-human running changes.

"Uh, and hello..."

"Will...Meyerhofer."

"Right. ”

Big smile. Wink at Jorge. And he's gone.

Yeah, that was humiliating. Seems deserving of a prize.

That's it for the Annals of Lameness – at least this year's edition. Maybe next time I'll award myself something for Lifetime Achievement.

You might not like awards shows. Or maybe this column seems like an excuse for me to bitch about law firm stuff that happened years ago. In psychotherapy sometimes you do that – bitch about stuff that happened years ago. Traumatic stuff. You might wrap it in humor, but it has a serious side, too. You put it into words, and process it, and you feel better.

Thanks for listening.

I Get It

My lawyer clients often come to me because, they say, I get it. I've been there – I'm a lawyer and I put in time at a big firm. I probably share that with you.

With some of my clients, I share more. I've Jew-bonded, gay-bonded, Harvard-bonded, NYU-bonded, Sullivan & Cromwell-bonded and dog-owner-bonded many, many times.

But there's more to it than that – more to "getting it" than attending the same institutions or sharing identities.

The question is worth asking. What? What do I get? What does "getting it" really mean?

Theoretically, any therapist ought to be able to work effectively with any client. That's because our job, to some extent, is to be a blank screen. We sit and listen, so you can feel heard and understood. As we listen, you grow to better understand yourself. I might not be a Cameroonian prince – but one of my clients was, so in the time we worked together, I learned a bit about the rules and contours of his world. I imagine he did, too.

Over the years, I've treated clients with past experiences I can only imagine – experiences like a life-threatening disease, the death of a spouse or violent rape.

Being a lawyer doesn't look or sound much like a life-threatening disease, the loss of a spouse or violent rape. In fact, to plenty of people, it doesn't sound bad at all.

I think that's the issue. That's why lawyers are so grateful that "I get it." Because to plenty of other people, it looks like lawyers have it pretty good.

So what do I get?

I get that being a lawyer can be an awful experience.
One of my clients said this to me the other day. She'd just had her first appointment with me, and was complaining about another therapist she'd seen.

"I told her all about the firm, and the life I was leading, but she just didn't get it. I could see it in her face – she was thinking, you're exaggerating, it probably isn't that bad."

I have worked in a big firm, and I know – it can be that bad. It can be downright horrendous.

I also know: **The money doesn't make it all okay.**
Another client told me she called an old friend of hers from home, in tears, and broke down about the terrible experience of working at her firm.

Her friend sounded sympathetic, but – as my client put it, "She was trying, but I knew she thought I was crazy. After all, she's earning about $40k as a school teacher, and I'm making $160k. What she's really thinking is how much money I'm making."

I used to earn a hefty law firm salary, and I know from experience it doesn't make everything okay. Not when you never leave the office except to sleep, never hear a word of thanks or praise for your work, and have work piled on that you don't know how to do when you're totally exhausted and you are expected to cancel your entire weekend on a moment's notice to try to figure out how to do it and all you want to do is close your office door and cry but you don't even have your own office.

I know how bad it can be. I have been there, and done that.

On the other hand, there are aspects of what's god-awful about a legal career that I didn't get until I sat and listened.

I graduated from a fairly top-tier school and went to a big-name white-shoe firm. I also incurred only moderate debt, because my father died when I was a teenager and left life insurance that helped pay for educating my brothers and myself. I also quit practicing law over a decade ago.

Thanks to these factors, there are some things I never experienced – and had to learn from my clients. Such as:

- You can graduate from a decent law school after working hard for three years and find yourself without a job and unsure how to get one.
- You can graduate from almost any law school with debt approaching two hundred and forty thousand dollars – an amount so large even a big firm salary hardly makes a dent in it.
- You can graduate from a decent law school and end up working as a "contract attorney" doing mindless document review, in a dark cellar, paid by the hour.
- On the other end of the spectrum, you can make partner and not enter paradise. You can find yourself under crushing pressure to bring in steady business and subjected to humiliating treatment if you fail. (Partners rarely express sympathy for associates and contract attorneys. I haven't noticed much affection flowing the other way, either. But it is my job to "get it" - to get all of it.)

So that's what I do. I take my experiences, and I listen to the experiences recounted to me each week, and I do my best to understand.

That's what it means, I think - to "get it."

You Sound Angry

One comment I hear frequently with regard to my columns is that I sound angry.

True enough. That's because I am angry.

I have no problem with anger. You're angry too. We all are, all the time. The problem isn't anger - it's perfectly natural, and can be a clarifying, inspiring force. Martin Luther King, Jr. was angry - righteously angry - about Jim Crow and the oppression of African-American people in the United States. The key is what he did with that anger.

If you go into action on unconscious anger, bad things can happen. You can act out, and have a tantrum, or hurt someone. Or you can act in, and bottle up, close down, isolate and disappear.

But if you own your anger, and put it into words, you can change the world. That's what Dr. King did, and Gandhi and Harvey Milk and a lot of my personal heroes.

In my case, I'd be happy if I could change the world of Biglaw.

Why am I so angry? Consider what I do for a living.

Each week I receive comments, emails and phone calls from victims of the law school/law firm complex. You know the drill: you get good grades in college, don't know what to do with yourself, want to please mom and dad, think a J.D. will be an "extremely versatile degree," sign up, borrow a small fortune and figure you'll work the details out later, once you pass the bar.

A few years go by, and you appear at my door, battered and bleeding, plop down in my chair and have a good cry.

I listen. I tolerate your feelings, and let you know you have a right to them. I don't offer solutions. I offer support.

That's what therapists do – we give you a place to listen to yourself, so you can grow more conscious, and maybe make changes that will help you to live a more authentic and happy life.

There isn't much I can do about your $200k in loans, or the vicious cruelty of law firms and the exploitation of the billable hour. My best advice is to remove yourself from a toxic environment, maintain emotional insulation, and learn techniques to provide self-care and self-soothing.

But I can't make the debt go away. And that's probably what's keeping you at the damned firm. You could probably figure out on your own that you need to get away from it, if you weren't handcuffed to your desk by those loans.

My broader point isn't about what I can or cannot do to help you – it's that the whole situation seems so pointless. I feel like Hawkeye Pierce, in MASH, when the helicopters show up bearing bleeding young people, and he scrambles into the operating tent to do his best to sew them back up and stanch the bleeding and even amuse himself by trying to laugh at the whole situation.

What he really wants to do is scream. Because it's frustrating. Watching young lives devastated for no reason is extremely frustrating. And it makes me angry.

For the record, here is a manifesto – in a nutshell, what I'd change right now about the damned law school/law firm complex:

The People's Therapist's Manifesto:
1) **Law school class sizes must shrink, and third-tier schools should go out of business.** We're generating too many lawyers. The jobs don't exist – at very least, the salaries the kids in these law schools are expecting to receive don't exist. The flood of lawyers must stop. Society could use more of almost anything – teachers, social workers, musicians, artists, salesmen, engineers, physicists, chemists – but not more lawyers.
2) **Student loans must be dischargeable in bankruptcy** – otherwise banks will never stop and ask themselves if lending $200k to a 23 year old is a good idea.

3) **Law school tuitions must come down.** If the easy, not-dischargeable-in-bankruptcy loan money is cut off, this will happen on its own. Law students cannot be cash cows funding entire universities.

4) **Law students must be required to demonstrate at least one year of actual experience working at a law firm or other appropriate legal setting prior to admission.** That way, they'd have some idea what they're getting into.

5) **Labor laws must be drafted and passed by legislatures.** Just as they are for mines and factories, labor regulations must be put in place for law firms, limiting requirements for "billable hours." You cannot expect workers to put in sixty to eighty hour weeks as a requirement of employment. Even the medical profession has cracked down on this sort of abuse. It's time for lawyers to wake up and say "enough." Contract attorneys - those guys doing doc review in basements – should unionize and engage in collective bargaining for improved conditions.

6) **Young people need to smarten up.** They're starting to hear the stories, and even the most naïve must be feeling queasy signing for massive loans in this economy. We need to spread the truth about the law school scam, even if that means storming the ramparts of august institutions like the ABA and local bar associations.

That's what I've come up with so far. I'm sure many of you could usefully add to this list.

I sit almost every day, listening to hurt, angry, wounded victims of a system I've grown to hate. That's made me angry. I don't apologize for it. I do promise to own my anger, put it into words, and use my words to inspire action.

One valuable feature of anger: when you're angry, you tend to say what you really mean.

Crack is Wack

A friend of mine, another ex-lawyer, was bemoaning the current state of the legal profession over lunch.

"It's only getting worse. Every year, the law schools get bigger, lining up more willing victims, stuffing them into the machine, packing the classes, pumping more clueless young attorneys into a market over-saturated to the point of calamity."

I told him I wasn't worried. He looked at me like I was mad.

"It's a disaster. A gigantic fraud. Kids with $200k in loans can't find contract attorney work paralegals used to turn their noses up at."

I shrugged. No big deal.

I knew something he didn't. I'd lived through the crack epidemic.

Way back before the dawn of time, in 1990, I worked as a social worker for a foster care agency in the depths of Brooklyn. That was the era when crack was decimating African-American neighborhoods across New York City and the entire country. It was a grim time. We were dealing with a flood of children – infants – who tested positive for cocaine at birth. Eventually, most of those kids turned out fine, but we didn't know that then. Meanwhile, their parents were hooked on one of the cheapest, most addictive, most destructive drugs ever invented.

For a while, it looked like Armageddon – a proud, indomitable community had survived centuries of slavery, poverty and racial discrimination, only to fall victim to a deadly addiction.

Then, suddenly, it was over. Rates of crack use fell, the violence let up, and things returned to normal.

What happened?

In brief, people wised up. You don't have to be a genius to realize crack is bad for you – you only have to live in an affected neighborhood and look around. I remember walking through East New York and Brownsville, watching skeletal, zombie-like figures stagger past abandoned buildings and empty lots, seeking another fix. Those were horrifying images – and eventually they did the trick. Every kid in the neighborhood knew someone who had used crack and was transformed into one of those walking corpses. The connection sank in: use crack, end up like that.

Back to law.

I work with a steady stream of clients who are graduating law school right now with staggering, mind-blowing, other-worldly levels of debt. I mean, like close to a quarter of a million dollars at the age of 26. And they don't have jobs, either. Or if they have jobs, their start dates are being delayed.

These people have little brothers, and kid sisters. They also have friends, who might be considering law school. All of these folks have eyes. Young people can recognize unhappiness – they can figure out going to law school might not be all that – that it might be something to avoid.

Just like the crack epidemic, the law epidemic will end once the truth is out. You can't hide masses of unemployed, unhappy, exploited law students. They can't be swept under the rug. Eventually, the shame will wear off, and they'll start telling their story – proclaiming it as a truth others ought to hear.

Within a few years, enrollment at the law schools will decline – especially at the second and third tier schools, many of which have been using their obscene profits to fund entire universities. They're going to have to find another way to produce money, because young people are smartening up, and they will rebel. This fraud can't last forever.

Eventually, the cycle will pass, and the number of students graduating with JD's and taking the bar exam will diminish. The profession will settle back into some semblance of normality.

Everything will work itself out. Just like it did in Brooklyn back in 1990.

Crack is wack. So is law.

People aren't that stupid.

Down off the Ledge

It's no secret my years at a big law firm were some of the unhappiest of my entire life. If I haven't gone into all the details, it's because there's some stuff so awful you're afraid, if you return to the memory, somehow you'll end up stuck there again.

It's been a long time. Nonetheless, I vividly recall – like it was yesterday - lying, curled in a fetal position, on the floor of my studio apartment downtown, gasping for what felt like hours with silent, wracking sobs, literally trembling with anxiety. This happened a few times (Sunday nights in particular were a horror show.) Those memories are a milestone of a sort – a lifetime low-water mark, a time I never wish to return to, under any circumstances – a bit like the "bottom" alcoholics talk about hitting and never wanting to revisit.

My dog, a skye terrier named Margaret, would trot over to see if she could help. She wouldn't even try to lick me – I was too far gone for that. She'd just nestle down nearby – making sure some of her warm furry body was pressed up against mine - and offer sympathy with big brown eyes.

In her own gentle way, Margaret talked me down off the ledge a few times. Once I'd cried myself out, I'd scoop her in my arms and climb into bed for a few hours sleep – blissful oblivion – before I had to face that law firm again.

Yes, there were times I wished I never had to wake up. That's as far as it went, but that happened.

Those vivid, painful memories – sobbing curled up on the floor – come back sometimes when I'm working with clients.

Okay, let's get real. "Working with clients" is a bit of a euphemism in this context - what I mean is, this stuff comes back when a client calls during an anxiety attack, writhing in agony the way I used to, and I'm doing my best to talk him off the ledge.

I do this a lot – talk lawyers through white-knuckled anxiety attacks. If you've experienced one of these, you know what I'm talking about. If you haven't been through it, please keep reading - but do so respectfully, because you cannot imagine how awful it feels.

So the question is *why*? Why does law trigger anxiety? And why does anxiety feel so goddamn awful?

I'm asked this stuff every week by lawyers trying to figure out what's happening to them – and why it's happening to them – and why it feels worse than anything they've ever felt before.

Essentially, this kind of anxiety reproduces the feeling that you're going to die. If you really want to go there, it's the feeling of an infant abandoned in the cradle. You are going to die because you have failed to please, and no one wants you and no one wants to care for you because you failed, and you are no good and now you are all alone and as a result, you will die.

That sounds absurd – infantile, Freudian rubbish, right? But stop, and think it through.

When lawyers try to describe their anxiety attacks, they tell me they feel trapped, like the water's climbing over your head and you can't breathe. There's more work and more work and you don't know how to do it and they email you more work it's late you need to sleep can't think straight more work they don't care it's complicated have to figure it out have to think stay up stay awake figure this out *fuck* can't figure this out. And then you're sitting in an empty office at 2 am on Sunday night, shaky, eyes red, feeling sweaty and a little sick and staring at some complicated thing you don't know how to do but no one cares they said do it but you can't figure out what they want you're just trying to stay awake and breathe try to breathe stay awake you want to curl up and cry but you have to figure this out and try to breathe...

Something like that.

In physical terms, anxiety tightens you up so you can't breathe, or sit still, or breathe, or sit still, or think, or sit still, or breathe or think or sit still or breathe...You want to jump out of your body. You want to not be in your body – not *be* you – to go away someplace where this fucking awful feeling stops. You feel your chest tightening, and that god-awful feeling like a cold steel ball in your chest, and you want to cry and then it starts and you hold on for dear life and hope it will stop.

The closest analog to extreme anxiety is extreme nausea – waves of agonizing nausea, like you're seasick in the hold of a ship on a lurching ocean and it smells like puke. Or pain - unrelenting, immobilizing pain, like you bang your leg and it hurts like hell - damn! - but then it keeps hurting and - what's going on? – it won't stop hurting and hurts worse and it's pounding it hurts so bad and it's freaking you out.

Yeah, I've been there. I know.

And if you're thinking – jeez, dude, man up, enough with the drama - then consider: I talk to lawyers experiencing strong anxiety from their jobs just about every week. And these are not wusses, or pussies or flakes and it's not limited to greenhorn juniors. These are serious-minded people, mid-level and senior associates, and – yes – partners. These guys have been in law for a while, but at some point it catches up with them, and the panic gets too close, and the walls feel like they're closing in.

What to do? Okay – here's my bag of tricks.

For most people, the impulse is to find a pill, something quick to make this feeling go away. You want it to stop, now, so you can catch your breath and try to figure out what's happening.

Pill-wise, the easiest fix is an anti-anxiety drug, a benzo like Klonopin, or Xanax. Longer term, some people end up on an anti-depressant, too, like Lexipro or Zoloft. I'm not a psychiatrist, and these aren't my speciality, but I respect your right to reach for quick relief. At very least, grabbing for a benzo beats grabbing for a bottle of vodka, which is what plenty of lawyers wind up doing.

But drugging yourself isn't much of an answer, is it? The best thing I've found for quick relief from anxiety – and I'm serious here – is physical exercise. If you're about to jump out of your skin and have the time and the will-power, go for a 30 minute run. Even a slow jog. Anything that raises your heart rate for 30 minutes will to leave you feeling better – and with anxiety, the rule is that any better automatically counts as a lot better.

Longer-term relief? We both know you have to get out of that firm. If, right now, you're panting for breath and fighting the impulse to break into sobs, you probably aren't arguing. The problem is how to get out. Switching jobs isn't a breeze in this economy, especially not in law, and you have loans up the wazoo. Any job hunt is going to take at least a few weeks and you're freaking out right now.

Okay, so we need something more – we need a plan for right now. To address anxiety – really address it - you need to climb into your own head, and start taking control over your thoughts.

It helps to enunciate the fear – the predictive thought that lies at the heart of all anxiety. Ask yourself – what's the worst that can happen? Something along the lines of failing, being told you're not committed, or not capable, not living up to expectations, and getting kicked out and left without a job, without money, without status, without respect – a total, forgotten loser, a person other people would rather not worry about. That's the abandonment fantasy.

So confront this fantasy. Is it true? If so, do you care? At this point, really - *do you care*? I used to tell myself – no kidding, I truly did this – that I'd rather be a waiter somewhere, or a prep cook, preferably in a nice, friendly vegan restaurant, and live in a little rented room in darkest Queens, then ever – ever - *ever, ever, ever* – work in a law firm again. There was no way I was going through *this* - this god-awful feeling of an anxiety attack, ever again. And I meant it. I didn't care about the money or the status or what my family thought or my friends – I was taking care of me. I couldn't live that way.

Which gets me to the real best weapon against anxiety. When you're having an anxiety attack, you're being reduced to your most primitive place of fear – like a tiny animal cornered by a predator. It's fight or flight, and you're looking for a means of escape and not finding anything.

So fight instead. Get your mojo back. Don't let those motherfuckers do this to you. You're a person – a damned smart person, and a good lawyer. You have value. You went to college and law school and worked your ass off. You're a nice person and you have friends and people who care about you. You care about yourself. This is *a job* – a stupid, punishing, exploitative *job*. They can ruin your social life, work you nights and weekends – but don't let them crush your heart, don't let them squash the fight out of you.

I will never, ever forget how bad it got. I promised myself, no matter how many years went by, and how far away and distant it all seemed in retrospect – I would never minimize the awful times.

I also promised I would never let it happen again. I shall never be treated that way, not one more time, in my entire lifetime. I promised that, and I mean it.

I talked myself down off the ledge. Now I talk others down, as best I can. I'm never going back to that place, ever. Not ever.

A Supposedly Fun Job I'll Never do Again

I'm at the Mandarin Oriental Hotel, on Columbus Circle, in New York City. I have a bias against fancy hotels. Consciously, this is because I'm too cool for pretentious places like this – I'd rather go to a smaller hotel that's savvy and tasteful. Unconsciously (it may be argued) I resent hotels like this because I can't afford them. Like flying business class (which I've only ever done once, with a law firm paying) the fancy hotel thing is a topic I feel a bit "sour grapes" around. But anyway.

I'm stepping into an elevator with my husband, or partner, or whatever euphemism you care to employ for my gay...whatever he is. The music, or muzak, is oriental - koto- or flute-infused Buddha Bar chillout fare. You're not supposed to say "oriental" because it implies they're Eastern and you're Western and you're choosing the directions. It's "Asian." But the hotel is still called "Oriental," which opens up issues. I'm wondering if my life partner - or whatever he is - is thinking the same thing. But anyway.

This is the Sullivan & Cromwell alumni reception and I'm nervous. My mind is racing in circles. I'm nervous in part because for a couple years I've been seeing partners at law firms as clients, so now I know the secret reason why S&C hosts these things. It's not a reunion like a high school reunion, for the heck of it – although private high school reunions aren't for the heck of it either, they're arranged by the development office to raise money. Sullivan & Cromwell throws these reunions – the *real* reason – so the partners can schmooze S&C alumni (former associates) with powerful in-house jobs at major corporations, and hit them up for work.

So why did they invite me? I don't have a real job or even anything resembling a real job. God willing, I'll never in my life hire a lawyer who charges more than a couple thousand bucks, and that'll be to buy an apartment some day. But S&C has no way to filter people with real jobs from people like me. It would be awkward to create a "do not invite" list of people (like me) who are of no use to them. To some degree, they're counting on someone like me – who left S&C with my tail between my legs and never did law again – to have the dignity not to show up (and if I do show up, to act like I'm doing what I'm doing – crashing a party for free food – and lay low.)

The food is pretty awesome, but I'll get to that later. My husband (or whatever he is) is Chinese, so food is a factor here, not to be taken lightly. But anyway.

The other reason I'm here – my "secret reason" - is that I'm THE PEOPLE'S THERAPIST, who has been publicly dissing poor S&C in my blog and on AboveTheLaw.com for the past year or two. So I should show up at this thing in order to...hmmm...why?

I have to be here. I sense that. I know it for certain, at some primitive, instinctive level. I need to show I'M NOT AFRAID. But of course, I am afraid, because I'm standing in this elevator with wealthy powerful WASP'y S&C people – people I remember from a dozen years ago when I worked at S&C and they took me to places like that Westchester country club where I met people like this. And of course, they are all in suit and tie, and I'm in what I use when I need to reproduce suit and tie (and it's spring or summer), which is a pair of linen pants from Banana Republic and a cornflower blue shirt and a blue linen jacket a friend gave me because it didn't fit him anymore.

I'm a therapist. I don't own a suit. I haven't worn a tie since a couple years ago, when I dug one out for a lesbian friend's 50th birthday. You don't mess with lesbians when they ask you to wear a tie – you just wear a tie. But I can't see spending $600 I don't have at Century 21 on a suit when I never wear suits. In fact, in the summer, as a therapist, I wear shorts and a polo shirt. That's a good thing about being a therapist.

So, I'm nervous and jittery and rattling on about nothing to my poor boyfriend (or whatever.) The lady on the 36th floor where the reunion is being hosted (it's a big space with floor to ceiling windows overlooking Central Park) manages (to my relief) to locate our name tags, which are kind of cool – they're magnetic, so you stick one over your suit chest pocket and slide another magnet inside the pocket and the whole mess stays on without poking a hole. A cool improvement over the old technology – I will never again intentionally use an old pin-type name tag.

And we're in the big room and there's Rodge Cohen, looking a bit older and even shorter than I remember. I poke my whatever he is in the ribs and whisper - "that's the head of the firm," and he shrugs. It always seemed impossible for someone who looks like Rodge Cohen to be the head of the whole place (or it used to be – officially, they have another guy now.) Rodge is...very small. And – at least in my mind's eye – well, okay, when I try to picture Rodge Cohen, I see Mr. Burns, from the Simpsons. That's unfair – he probably doesn't look like Mr. Burns, but if I'm being honest, that's the image that comes to mind. Sorry, Rodge.

We circulate and it becomes obvious the food is going to require some serious attention. There is a lot of eating we need to do. My hubby focuses his attention, quite sensibly, on the sushi, and we begin to graze. A partner wanders over and chats us up, which is absurd, since we're so obviously not the people he's supposed to be chatting up. But he's a tax partner, so maybe he's clueless and doesn't know better than to chat us up. Or maybe he sees my name tag and realizes I'm THE PEOPLE'S THERAPIST. Or maybe he's just gay and sees me with my boyfriend - or whatever he is – and decides we'd be fun to bond with. By the end of the evening we will have mostly talked to gay people - in fact, mostly to gay men. It will become weird how gay this party is - and sort of a relief, since gay people seem less scary, maybe because we're gay, or maybe because gay people seem less scary to most people.

The tax partner doesn't seem to know or care that I'm THE PEOPLE'S THERAPIST, but he does seem to be gay, and pretty nice and we chat and then he drifts away, which is kind of a relief, since we have a major plate of sushi to consume and have been waiting awkwardly for him to stop schmoozing so we can eat it. He's followed by another partner, but this guy is the real deal, a fairly important one whose name I remember and this guy quickly realizes his mistake, and catches on that we're nobody worth schmoozing and that there's an enthusiasm gap since we're deep in food, and the place is starting to fill up, so he zips away to talk to someone with a name tag from a French bank or hedge fund or something like that.

Back to eating. And more eating. I propose we try the Chinese food – the spring rolls are good. We nab a few shrimp dumplings and fall into a rhythm. Between bites, I inform my *whatever* that this is nothing – in the old days it was *totalement* over the top. When S&C was really S&C, there was *the mountain of oysters*. That was the signature dish, the *pièce de résistance*.

It is especially disappointing not to see *the mountain of oysters*, since I have been talking up *the mountain of oysters* to my whatever for weeks, as a hook to get him to accompany me to this thing. I didn't want to do it alone (although I did do it alone a few years ago, at the last reunion, when my whatever was stuck at the office, but that time I only stayed for a half hour because we had free tickets to a Broadway show and I was supposed to meet him there. That time they still had *the mountain of oysters*, perhaps the *final* mountain of oysters ever. Oh well.)

The mountain of oysters? Let me explain: There was a time, back *in my day*, when, even at the monthly attorney get-togethers down in the attorney dining room, they put out a heap of oysters – yes, a veritable *mountain*, on a silver tray - and you could stand there like a walrus and slurp them down and then some very nice man in a toque would put out more. They had peeled shrimp, too – a *mountain* of peeled shrimp – but that was kind of the runner-up attraction. Sadly, the *mountain of oysters* is now little more than the embodiment of an S&C long-gone.

Another thing I notice: the champagne has changed. I'm drinking diet coke tonight – lots of diet coke – but diet coke nonetheless, because I don't want to get tipsy at this thing, or drunk, surrounded by S&C partners. Later on, though, like ten minutes before we leave, I order champagne to see what happens, and – sure enough – it's no longer *Veuve Clicquot* like it was in my day – it's some shabby *blanc de blanc*. I mean, c'mon.

We decide to *circulate*. It's not a very promising crowd – lots of those very serious-looking white people in suits with that "worth a lot of money" expression on their faces. But I spot a gay partner whom I remember (I even worked on a deal with him once), and he's there with his Chinese boyfriend (or whatever) and we head over that way and stand next to them and I look for a way into the conversation. They basically ignore me, so I finally say "hi" and they say hi and the guy next to them strikes up a conversation with me and it turns out he's gay too – he keeps talking about his "partner" and initially I don't know if that's supposed to mean he's a partner at a law firm (his name tag doesn't say S&C) or something more *sodomical*, but eventually I catch his (gay) drift and he seems like a nice guy and he used to be at S&C (of course) but now he works in e-discovery, or something complicated having to do with e-discovery. He and the gay partner have pretty much worn out the conversational theme of "my gosh, you (the S&C partner and his whatever) just bought a weekend place all the way up in the *Berkshires* – that's so far away." The conversation's more awkward subtext emerges, which is that they're insanely rich, and have a vacation house that's almost certainly fabulous beyond all reckoning - and we wish we had one, too. My whatever and I don't possess a vacation house – or even own an apartment. It's possible that up-state gay dream houses are another topic I feel a bit "sour grapes" around – and, to judge from the look on Mr. e-discovery's face, I might not be alone on that score.

In any case, the gay S&C partner and his Chinese whatever were never terribly friendly back in the day, and they still aren't. After we drift away from this conversational enclave, my whatever whispers something along the lines of "what's got into *that* queen!?" and I realize he's talking about the Chinese whatever – the S&C partner's Chinese whatever - and he's feeling a little miffed that one Chinese whatever would treat another Chinese whatever with such *hauteur*, which in English translates quite rightly as "attitude."

We drift pass the Italian buffet – cheese, antipasto, pasta, another pasta, risotto. There's also a beef tenderloin being conspicuously sliced by an eager-looking guy in an apron. As a pescatarian (who would likely be a vegetarian if my whatever weren't an omnivorous Cantonese and I weren't the type to compromise to make a relationship work) I feel obligated to look away and ignore it and remind you a tenderloin is a cow's butt cheek (although I'm aware of the hypocrisy in this attempt to gross you out coming from someone who eats fish and who, even if he *were* vegetarian, would probably classify everything on the food chain from oysters on down as a vegetable.) The whole ceremony involved in finding a plate and a knife and fork and sitting down to tenderloin seems like a commitment, and there are few takers, which is probably why the guy looks so eager.

I'm starting to feel less stressed out and a bit more, well, bored. I strike up a conversation with one of the few black people at this thing, an attractive young woman. I happen to have noticed, with an acuity that can only be described as homosexual, that she is rockin' out some fishnets, tastefully hidden away under a knee-length skirt, but still, there be fishnets down there and some fierce pumps and I'm impressed and I say as much to her, and of course she works in fashion and loves it. Her date turns out to be a guy who's still friendly with one of the few people I actually liked at S&C when I was there and we chat away and things warm up a bit or de-frost, and it starts to feel like a party, or even a *par-tay,* a little bit. This guy, her date, is African, and I remember him now – he left right after I did, and ended up working for the World Bank or something like the World Bank that sounds equally cool and impressive.

The only reason we're here chatting is, of course, S&C - so at some point when we run out of other stuff to talk about, we make a game of pointing at some of the oldest, crustiest, scariest S&C partners and trading stories. We don't have anything substantive to say about them – mostly it devolves into pointing and laughing and making shit up.

Me: "That guy, the tall, bald one, he's a motherfucker. I swear, he's like the head of the evil committee. He's truly scary."

African guy: "Oh, yes. I remember him well." (Chuckle.)

That kind of thing. I couldn't help thinking it was a bit like gazing through glass in the reptile house at the zoo, staring at something coiled and venomous, and chuckling to reassure yourself it can't hurt you. I'd cuddle a sleeping cobra as soon as I'd strike up conversation with the head of litigation at S&C - I'm not going anywhere near the sonofabitch and neither is the African guy. Who are we kidding?

At some point we run out of steam and drift apart, and and then things quiet down in the room and someone from S&C – some partner I don't remember existing - starts talking into a mic from a podium set up at the back of the room, with the windows and Central Park behind him. He goes on about how this is a tradition they've been honoring for a long time and how one year the reunion was canceled because of a massive snow storm and how for the first time this year they've invited an S&C alum to speak. Then he introduces an alum who's now the dean of – I think I heard it right – *West Virginia* Law School. Like, there's a law school in *West Virginia*? Like West Virginia *needs* a law school? One more third tier factory pumping out lawyers.

The dean guy starts talking and it's a jovial commencement-type speech – he's comparing securities law to particle physics – in both you talk with false assurance about something no one really understands, blah blah blah. He looks the part of a dean, graying at the temples, like a beloved headmaster at Groton or Deerfield. It turns out he had an amazing experience at S&C. It was a brilliant preparation for yadda yadda.

My whatever leans over and whispers: "If he left S&C, doesn't that mean he had to leave? He didn't make partner?" A greater awareness dawns. "But then – all these people – if they're not partners, they're the one's who didn't make partner, right? They all had to leave?"

I nod. My unflappable, down-to-Earth, no-bullshit Chinese *whatever* has figured it out – put two and two together and cut to the chase. "S&C alum" means you got kicked out – you didn't make partner.

I explain further: "This dean guy is kissing ass with the partners. He's hoping they'll take the editor of the West Virginia law review as a summer associate. I don't see it happening. I mean - get real."

I ponder that transaction. A speech offered in the desperate hope S&C will hire a kid from West Virginia Law School. My guess is most of the classes departing their hallowed halls during the past few years would kill for a doc review gig at twenty-five an hour. Meanwhile, the hundred and seventy thousand each one owes in school loans should guarantee their beloved dean a comfortable life.

The speech is impossible to follow. I try, but I can't. I'm pre-occupied with picturing that hypothetical conversation in my head, wondering how close it actually got to an S&C partner saying – "you give a speech, maybe we'll take one of your kids."

The speech peters out, and that's it – no more mic and podium. We return to wandering around the room. I become conscious of the fact that we've been sticking to a counter-clockwise pattern of rotation. Three full cycles so far.

Over by the sushi, a youngish guy walks up to me and says "hey, you're the guy from AboveTheLaw."

"Yeah," I say, secretly flattered – in fact, SECRETLY THRILLED – but unsure where this is going.

"I want to talk to you about that, I mean seriously."

"Sure."

He settles next to me with a drink.

"Don't you think, I mean, S&C did okay by us, considering?" He hesitates, in a young, clueless, self-conscious way, and his eyes scan the room. There are S&C partners on the prowl like circling sharks. "S&C taught me a level of seriousness, a commitment to getting it right, down to the tiniest detail."

I know what he means. The seriousness of the place. The sense they are the best law firm in the world. I guzzled that Kool-Aid too.

"Yeah. But it was one of the worst experiences of my life. They destroyed me physically and emotionally. How'd you make out?"

His reply is quick: "Yeah. Sure. It was bad."

"How bad?"

He avoids my gaze, staring down at the floor, like he's making sure it's still there.

"Oh, yeah. Bad." He takes a hurried sip of his drink. His hand looks shaky.

I decide I've made my point. He's in banking now, apparently as of five minutes ago. He just switched jobs - probably quit S&C and received the "alumni" invitation in the mail the next day. He looks green, lost, young, traumatized. I hand him my card.

As soon as we're alone, my Chinese whatever comments: "That guy's just saying that stuff. He looks scared. He's young, huh?"

At some point I graze the dessert table (my whatever pointedly doesn't, so as not to encourage me.) Then I wander around the room a bit more, stare out the window at Central Park, then simply gaze at faces that seemed deeply scary when I was thirty-one years old. They still seem deeply scary. I remind myself I never had a worse time in my life than I had working for them – but it was a long time ago. There's comfort in how long ago and I bathe in that comfort.

It's getting near the end of this shindig, and it still isn't clear if anyone (other than the young guy and the gay partner) knows who I am – either recognizes the anonymous junior associate from twelve years ago, or spots THE PEOPLE'S THERAPIST. I've got shark metaphors on the brain by this juncture and find myself running a mental comparison between one particular heavyweight senior partner and a patrolling hammerhead. His admittedly widely-spaced eyes connect with mine and he flashes teeth. Was that a glimmer of malice? Has he caught a whiff of chum? My mind could be playing tricks. A moment later he's huddled with a bald guy with clown-like patches of white hair over his ears. I vaguely connect the clown guy to long-ago CLE luncheon meetings.

Now it's time to leave. I told my whatever we'd stay an hour. We stayed almost two, and the crowd's thinning. It's raining outside. We grab two of the free S&C umbrellas, which the whatever *loves*. They're free, and have "real wood" handles. Nice. We exchange looks, but no, we're not grabbing an extra one – too public, and too potentially embarrassing.

Just kidding. We don't steal extra free umbrellas because we're not *those* kind of people.

A guy turns to me in the elevator down.

"You're that guy who wrote that column, right?"

"Uh... yeah." I notice his name tag says "Sullivan & Cromwell." That means he's still there. That means he's a partner. Eek.

"Interesting," he says. Which doesn't mean anything, but isn't overtly hostile either. In fact, he's around my age and seems a bit flirty. It turns out he's gay, too, (I mean is *everyone* at this thing gay?) His inclinations come to light when I mention the gay partner with the Chinese whatever. It turns out this guy has a Chinese whatever, too – in London. Unbelievable. (Is *everyone* at this thing a gay guy with a Chinese whatever?)

We shake hands at the subway entrance (he's not taking the subway) and I flightily propose a gathering of gay S&C lawyers with Chinese whatevers. He laughs and says "I have your card." Oh, yeah, I forgot - I gave him my card at some point. I wonder if that means he'll call. He doesn't.

Later, in the subway, my Chinese whatever is musing: "I see all this tonight and I think I should have gone to law school." He sighs wearily. "I should have worked at Sullivan &Cromwell, had that success."

I'm exasperated. Has he read my columns? Has he heard nothing during our seven years together? How many times have I described the hell I went through in Biglaw, and the hell I see my clients going through now at these places...

I say most of this aloud, and he replies: "They didn't seem that bad."

"Yeah, well it's not like they're all Adolf Hitler, but then you didn't have to work for them."

He mulls this over, and I drop it. I know – and I adore him for this – my whatever's thinking about the view of Central Park from the 36th floor of the Mandarin Oriental, and the open bar, and all those preppy white people in suits, exuding money and privilege. Keep in mind, my Chinese whatever emigrated from Hong Kong when he was eleven, and for much of his teens shared a windowless basement bedroom in Bensonhurst with his grandmother and bagged groceries after school and weekends to help support the family. He's got a good job now – earns more than I do – but he could have done with a little Sullivan & Cromwell glamor in the course of his life. I'm not holding it against him if he's dazzled.

They put on their game face. They showed their stuff. I showed up, and we had a stare-off. I think it was a draw.

S&C throws these reunions every five years or so. I guess I'll keep coming. I'll see how I feel in another five years – and whether I get invited.

SUMMATION

I ran the idea for this book past a couple of literary agents a while back – nice, smart, competent people, who know the book business inside and out. They hated it.

They told me no one wanted to read a book about lawyers except lawyers – and no lawyer wanted to read a book that was "negative" about being a lawyer.

Nonetheless, my column in AboveTheLaw was a hit, so there had to be a book. They proposed a title like "How to be a Happy Lawyer."

Ironically, a few months later someone sent me a link to Amazon, with the news that "How to be a Happy Lawyer" (or something darn close) already exists. According to the comments on Amazon, it's a combination of bland lawyer-specific advice and watered-down self-help cliches.

I couldn't write How to be a Happy Lawyer. Instead, I wrote this.

I am a lawyer – or was a lawyer – or whatever - and I can't lie about an experience that left me a mental and physical wreck.

This is serious. The "profession" - as I laughingly call it – is falling apart. It has been for ages, but so long as people were finding jobs and getting paid we all ignored that fact.

Now the bubble has popped. It is no longer a secret that using law school as a way to get your parents off your back will only land you in debt up to your eyebrows and hating life. Wealth and power have to be earned the old-fashioned way – by working for it, not copping out and blowing a wad on grad school.

If you're already in Biglaw hell, I don't have a lot of easy answers – but at least it helps to own the situation.

Good therapists go easy on offering advice – tough problems don't lend themselves to pat, easy answers. You can find your own, better solutions yourself. Good therapists concentrate instead on listening, and repeating back to you what they see and hear. The idea is to make you more aware, more conscious of what's going on.

That – to a large degree – is what this book is about: Consciousness.

Owning the situation.

I get it. I have been there, and I have done that.

I know how much it sucks. I also know you'll make it through, put it behind you, and move on to greener pastures.

In the meantime, I hope I've helped you to share a laugh at this mess you've gotten yourself into.

ACKNOWLEDGMENTS

First, profound apologies to some happy, successful dentist friends: William Nguyen, Jason Kim, Ellen Lee, Glenn Chiarello, JR Cassidy, Peter Farzin, and Demetrios Sengos. You bring talent and enthusiasm to your profession. You do important work. You improve the lives of others. We should all be so lucky.

My thanks to the brilliant staff of AboveTheLaw.com – especially Kashmir Hill, Elie Mystal and David Lat. I love you guys.

Steve Sendor helped out in innumerable ways with the preparation of this book. Many thanks to you, good friend, for coming through yet again.

Muchas gracias to my dear sister, Tania Garcia, for her expert advice during the preparation of this book for publication.

Another dear old friend, Christine Sullivan, created the beautiful cover for this book. Thank you, Christine, for sharing your extraordinary talent as an artist and designer.

My deepest gratitude and appreciation to the countless lawyers and others who have written letters and emails and posted comments to ThePeoplesTherapist.com – and to the dozens of you who have shown up at my office door and shared your stories as we worked together in psychotherapy. You made this book possible.

As always, much gratitude to my long-suffering life-partner, William Yan To Kwok, for his patience and equanimity as I hammered out these columns and assembled this book. How shall I put this? I love you.

ABOUT THE AUTHOR

Will Meyerhofer received his BA from Harvard, his JD from NYU School of Law and his MSW from the Hunter College School of Law. After law school, he worked as an associate doing corporate work at Sullivan & Cromwell LLP. *Then things changed.* He is now a psychotherapist in private practice in New York City.

CPSIA information can be obtained at www.ICGtesting.com
Printed in the USA
LVOW070333261011

252049LV00001B/89/P